DON'T WASTE
MY TIME

DON'T WASTE MY TIME

Expert Secrets for Meetings That Inspire, Engage, and Get Results

Kimberly Devlin

Trainers Publishing House
Seabrook Island, SC

Trainers Publishing House
www.trainerspublishinghouse.com
Email: info@trainerspublishinghouse.com

Ordering Information

Quantity Sales: sales@trainerspublishinghouse.com
Individual Sales: Amazon.com and Kindle.com

ISBN: 978-1-93924-711-7 (print)
ISBN: 978-1-93924-712-4 (ebook)

Trainers Publishing House:

Publisher: Cat Russo
Editorial Director: Jacqueline Edlund-Braun
Rights Associate and Data Manager: Nancy Silva
Marketing: Michelle Rabelle, IndigaMedia
Interior Design and Composition: Kristin Goble, PerfecType, Nashville, TN
Cover Design: Patty Sloniger Design, Houston, TX
Cover art: Fotolia

Contents

2 WHAT BELONGS ON THE AGENDA? 27
Seven Key Elements for Every Agenda

3 HOW DO I PREVENT BAD BEHAVIOR BEFORE
IT BEGINS?. 43
50+ Proactive Strategies to Avoid Meeting Meltdowns

"Time. How brief and fleeting your allotment of it."
—Marcus Aurelius

Let's Redefine What Meetings Can and Should Be

It has been said that a meeting is an event in which the minutes are kept and the hours are lost. Standing outside a conference room recently, I thought of this when a man inside the room opened the door, peered out, and asked if I had the room reserved. "Yes, I have it booked starting at 12:30," I said. His reaction was priceless—his face relaxed and he silently mouthed two words to me: "Thank you!" In the silence, his gratitude was palpable. My room reservation was about to force an end to the meeting he was enduring—and he couldn't have been more pleased.

It is no wonder, given their track records, that meetings make great material for humorists:

- Meetings are indispensable when you don't want to do anything. —*John Kenneth Galbraith*
- To get something done, a committee should consist of no more than three people, two of whom are absent. —*Robert Copeland*
- If you had to identify, in one word, the reason why the human race has not achieved, and never will achieve, its full potential, that word would be *meetings*. —*Dave Barry*

But, elusive as they may be, there *are* meetings that people want to come to, participate in eagerly, and leave feeling good about what was accomplished. Which do you want to be known for leading? The secrets to meetings that inspire, engage, and get results are not complicated. You just need to know what they are to be able to exert their powerful influence.

"One Size Fits All" Isn't Just a Lie on Clothing Labels

One size fits all is also a lie for meeting guidance. There is a foundational set of actions to achieve the promises of this book. There is not, however, a single prescribed path through them. With the guidance found here, you will need to make choices to suit the unique dynamics of your meetings, their goals, their participants, and other factors. No matter the size, purpose, or type of meetings you lead—whether you are convening multiple teams at a conference, leading a staff meeting, chairing a PTA committee, or facilitating a virtual meeting of remote workers—this book can help you get the results you need with the investment of just one hour from your busy schedule.

How Can This Book Help You Redefine Meetings?

People don't mind meetings—they mind meetings that waste their time.

That distinction is what led us at EdTrek, Inc. to create the training program *Don't Waste My Time*™, upon which this book is based. Both the course and the book:

- Reveal expert facilitation techniques
- Provide tools that streamline meeting preparation and follow-through
- Share strategies to manage the difficult situations and bad behaviors that perpetually plague meetings
- Support you in *using* all of this guidance.

Through your effective and consistent application of the strategies in this book, you will inspire meeting members instead of bore them, engage participants instead of speak to "attendees," and achieve real results instead of close meetings with hollow phrases such as "OK, I think that about does it," "Nice work," or—most dreaded of all—"We can finish this up next time."

Reading the book—just like attending the training—is only a first step. To achieve meetings that inspire, engage, and get results, you will need to refine your meeting preparation, approach, facilitation, and follow-up. Improving any one of these will be beneficial—mastering all of them will be essential to your success. *Don't Waste My Time* will help you get there.

If your team would benefit from practical, hands-on training for meetings that *Don't Waste My Time*, contact us at www.EdTrek.com.

Get Ready, Set, Go!

"You don't have to be great to start,
but you have to start to be great."
—*Zig Ziglar*

You are busy. You want better meetings—but who has the time? The *Smarter in an Hour* series is designed with you in mind. Commit 60 minutes to reading the core content of this book and you will be well on your way to saving hours and days—as well as ending untold human suffering around conference tables.

One Hour? Really?

Yes, you can read the core content of this book in an hour. In even less time, you can read the six One-Minute Roundup chapter summaries! For a deeper dive, you will want to explore all of the book's resources, worksheets, job aids, and online bonus content.

You have the book, you have an hour, now choose how you will use them to achieve meetings that inspire, engage, and get results:

❒ Read the core content of the six main chapters:
  - Chapter 1: 18 minutes to plan your meeting
  - Chapter 2: 9 minutes to prepare your agenda
  - Chapter 3: 13 minutes to prevent bad behavior proactively

- Chapter 4: 5 minutes to manage disruptive behavior reactively
- Chapter 5: 5 minutes to ensure follow-through with after-meeting actions
- Chapter 6: 10 minutes to apply this all to one-on-one meetings

❏ Start with the six One-Minute Roundup summaries that close the main chapters. Use your remaining 54 minutes to explore the areas most useful to you right now.

❏ Review the table of contents to choose the chapters aligned with your greatest pain points and dedicate your hour to their core content, sidebars, worksheets, job aids, quotes, and so on. And, to download the accompanying bonus content, visit www.KimberlyDevlin.com.

❏ Take a deep dive into Chapter 1—complete the worksheets, highlight the new strategies you will implement, assess your meeting strengths and weaknesses, read all of the sidebars as well as the bonus content available online at www.KimberlyDevlin.com.

❏ Jump around—it is your hour and your book—use them both as you see fit!

"If all you can do is crawl, start crawling."
—Rumi

What You Can Achieve With This Book and 60 Minutes

With this book and 60 minutes, you can achieve meetings that inspire, engage, and get results—regardless of which option you choose. Tick-tock—let's get to it!

Where Do I Begin?

Seven Strategies for Meetings That Inspire, Engage, and Get Results

"The only place success comes before work is in the dictionary."
—Vidal Sassoon

People don't like meetings for lots of reasons—they are boring, unproductive, exhausting, and lack structure—bottom line, meetings are often a waste of time. It isn't sufficient to reserve a room, send an appointment invitation via email, and show up expecting actively engaged participants and a productive event. There is a better way—and it starts with the PLANNER framework, described in this chapter. Although planning a meeting will take some of your time, not planning your meeting will *waste* everyone's time, including yours.

Take the Guesswork Out of Meetings!

You can run effective meetings every time—if you approach them with forethought. But what are the essential elements to planning a meeting that stays on track and gets the results that everyone wants? Great meetings are the result of planning based on Purpose, Location, Agenda, Names, Note-taking,

Expectations, and Responsibilities—the PLANNER framework. Including these seven factors transforms a gathering around a conference table or on a call into a collaborative environment in which individuals are inspired, everyone engages, and the team achieves results.

This chapter will look at each component of the framework in turn. Before reading on, complete Tool 1-1, which will enable you to compare your interpretation of PLANNER's components to the guidance provided in each section of the chapter. This insight will accelerate your meeting effectiveness quotient, putting you on the fast track to meeting successes.

PLANNER: Purpose

Think of a meeting you attended without having a clear understanding of what you were there to achieve. How would you characterize that experience? If you are like most people I've asked, your answer sounds like "frustrating," "infuriating," or "a waste of my time."

The antidote for frustrating, waste-of-time meetings? Purpose. Identifying the purpose of your meeting (the outcomes you want to achieve) is critical—and you probably already *know* that. It is in the *execution* of this action that many encounter problems. To gauge if you are at risk here, select an upcoming meeting you have scheduled and consider the reason you are holding it. Write down the purpose of your meeting in the space provided below.

My Meeting's Purpose

_____

_____

Your purpose may have room for improvement if what you wrote resembles any of the following:

- Discuss benefits and drawbacks of four employee benefits vendor proposals.
- Provide an overview of the new security protocols.

Tool 1-1: Your Starting Point for Meetings That Inspire, Engage, and Get Results

To get where you want to be, it helps to first know where you are. In support of that, take a moment to complete this worksheet. It identifies the seven components of the PLANNER framework, explained throughout this chapter. For each, jot down what you think it entails. If you think of actions associated with a component, include them. If you identify questions that need to be answered to plan a meeting, write them. The more detailed you are now, the better you will be positioned to improve your use of PLANNER to solve your meetings' challenges.

PLANNER Framework	My Impression of What This PLANNER Component Entails
Purpose	
Location	
Agenda	
Names	
Note-taking	
Expectations	
Responsibilities	

- Brainstorm strategies to resolve recent customer complaints.
- Consider best options to comply with required 20 percent budget cut.
- Review project progress and status of remaining open items.

Critique this list of meeting purposes. Why do they have room for improvement? What commonalities exist among them—and yours possibly? As written, will they inspire people to achieve them? How can they be enhanced to engage meeting members? And, how would you revise them to improve the meetings' results?

Now, compare them to these aligned examples that have been recast as outcomes:

First Drafts of Purpose Statements	Purpose Statements Recast as Outcomes
Discuss benefits and drawbacks of four employee benefits vendor proposals.	Ranked list of employee benefits vendor candidates.
Provide an overview of the new security protocols.	All employees following the new security protocols consistently and immediately.
Brainstorm strategies to resolve recent customer complaints.	Three lists of actions to resolve recent customer complaints, grouped by: under our control and implemented immediately, under our control and implemented within 30 days, and under our influence and pursued this quarter.
Consider best options to comply with required 20 percent budget cut.	Agreement on where to cut 20 percent from the budget.
Review project progress and status of remaining open items.	A project timeline with key milestones highlighted.

Are the differences just a matter of semantics or phrasing? Do they basically say the same thing? No. The revised purpose statements in the right column identify desired tangible or observable outcomes or *results* of the meeting; whereas, the first drafts in the left column describe *processes*. This is an important distinction, because it is possible to discuss, brainstorm, and consider options for hours and days without *achieving* anything. Outcomes make clear to all what they are there to accomplish.

With this in mind, reconsider your purpose statement and recast it here as a tangible or observable outcome. It may help you to remember that *processes* begin with verbs and *outcomes* begin with nouns.

My Meeting's Redefined Purpose

_____

_____

"You should never go to a meeting or make a telephone call without a clear idea of what you are trying to achieve."
—Steve Jobs

>>> **Reality Check:** If your Purpose is not well defined as outcomes— or not clearly communicated—you may hear any of the following during your meeting:

- "Why are we meeting, exactly?"
- "I think we have said all there is to say on this topic."
- "I'm sorry, but why are we discussing this?"
- "How much longer are we going to focus on this?"

>>> **Bottom Line:** The Purpose of your meeting should answer this question: What are we meeting to *accomplish*? It should be tangible or observable. And, it should be realistically achievable during the scheduled time for the meeting.

PLANNER: Location

Be honest—have you declined meeting invitations while saying to yourself "There is no way I am going *there* for a meeting!" With the demands on our time and the volume of meeting requests received, we are often looking for

Expert Secret:
How Many Outcomes Should I Have?

The magic number of outcomes for your meeting will depend on multiple factors. One outcome might be enough; and more than three to five may risk bringing on meeting fatigue. Remember, you want your meeting members to leave feeling energized, focused, and clear on next steps. Consider these factors when developing outcomes for your meeting:

- The visibility of your meeting goals organizationally—high-profile work may take more time.

- The scope of your meeting outcomes and how much effort will be required to achieve them.

- Your intended processes for achieving the meeting goals—the lengthier your processes, the fewer total outcomes your meeting can comfortably sustain.

- Participants' current familiarity with the task at hand or the issues related to it.

- Whether or not a facilitator will be enlisted to manage the meeting's processes—a skilled facilitator will keep the group on task, draw on practiced facilitative techniques, and provide clear direction to subgroups for complex processes, thereby enhancing meeting efficiency.

- Participants' tolerance for meeting fatigue—based on personality, position, current level of fatigue from meetings outside your control, or other factors.

- The relative priority participants place on the outcomes—in other words, how committed are they to the outcomes? Do they care?

When writing your outcomes, consider these factors to determine what is reasonable for meeting members to achieve in a single collaboration.

any reason to decline attending. Don't allow something so seemingly insignificant as the meeting location to derail your meetings' successes.

Here are some key factors to consider in choosing a meeting location:

- **Is the space conducive to achieving the meeting's purpose?** For example, a snug space with a large conference table dominating the room may work as a location to reach decisions on budget cuts but not when the group needs to chart, review, and categorize ideas to identify the best actions to resolve customer complaints.

- **What equipment and seating options may be required?** And are they available in the space?
- **Is there cachet or stigma associated with the space?** A location's reputation could work for or against you. Choose wisely.
- **Will your invited meeting members consider the location to be convenient?** The answer may not be obvious—or static. A space may be problematic at certain times—say due to traffic or other considerations—or attractive at others—as when key meeting members already have a standing meeting scheduled there. When you schedule for your participants' convenience, you can help streamline their day.
- **Does the location create a "home team advantage" for some participants?** When a meeting involves negotiations—developing contract terms, disparate groups or individuals coming to agreements, dividing responsibility between divisions or departments, and so on—a neutral location will establish an impartial environment in which to make decisions most productively and respectfully.
- **Are there costs associated with reserving the space?** Fixed rental fees are one cost; required catering and onsite parking may be others. Even though hard costs can be difficult to bear, soft costs such as eternal indebtedness for "borrowing our space" won't hit your budget but may force you to pay a higher price in other ways.

>>> **Reality Check:** Are you choosing meeting locations as indiscriminately as you do quick-pick lottery numbers? Is your preferred location for all meetings the physical or virtual location that is most convenient for you?

Expert Secret:
Virtual Meeting Considerations

What if your meeting is happening virtually, via Skype, Adobe Connect, GoToMeeting, or another platform? You want to think through the logistics of your virtual "location" too. For example, will participants need to download software in advance? Is the medium conducive to the number of participants, the participants' communication styles, the relationships between the parties, and so on?

Keep in mind these other practical considerations for virtual meetings:

- Will everyone be skilled at using the technology as intended?
- How will technological challenges be managed? And, by whom?
- What contingencies will be in place for bad connections, excessive background noise, difficulty hearing contributors on speaker phones, and so on?
- How will group work, decisions, and tabled items be recorded and displayed during the meeting?
- What will you do to ensure everyone's commitment to and focus on the meeting instead of multi-tasking?
- What techniques will ensure everyone's engagement throughout the meeting?

>>> **Bottom Line:** Choosing the wrong location can render an otherwise successful meeting a waste of time. Why? Key people may not come at all, the location's inadequacies may be distractions, attempts to overcome its shortcomings may be further distractions, participants may begin multi-tasking once the meeting's flow is interrupted, and key people may leave early when they recognize the meeting has become a waste of their time. It is a vicious cycle. Choose the *right* location—not the most convenient one.

PLANNER: Agenda

The agenda for your meeting is so critical that Chapter 2 is dedicated to it. For now, accept that you do need an agenda. A well-crafted agenda will be your playbook for the meeting. It will define for everyone the outcomes that are your meeting's purpose. It will specify the processes planned for achieving the outcomes. It will support you in proactively preventing tangents from surfacing. And it will demonstrate your preparedness for the meeting. Again, people don't mind meetings—they mind meetings that waste their time. Your preparation and distribution of a well-crafted agenda will engage people before your meeting even begins.

>>> **Reality Check:** Is an agenda a nicety or a necessity?

>>> **Bottom Line:** An agenda is hands-down a necessity.

PLANNER: Names

Here is a riddle: What happens in a meeting when the right people aren't there? The answer: Nothing—other than reinforcing the stereotype that meetings are a waste of time.

The meetings you want to be known for—inspiring, engaging, results-driven—require having the right people in them. This is a basic premise for meeting effectiveness but one that is commonly violated. To have the right people in the room, you need to shift your approach to extending invitations. Two common extremes are inviting everyone you can think of or attempting to fly beneath the radar by inviting as few as you can.

Avoid these extremes by following three simple steps. First, with your meeting outcomes defined, consider what each potential participant will *contribute* in support of achieving the goal. Here are a few examples of what the right participants can contribute:

- Share valued content based on experience or expertise.
- Commit resources—money, materials, people, or others.
- Approve plans developed during the meeting.
- Accept responsibility for next steps.
- Represent an otherwise under-represented perspective in the meeting. (This contribution can be critical in certain situations. Post-meeting power plays and political posturing by the

unrepresented can easily derail a meeting's accomplishments after the fact.)

- Facilitate the meeting's processes.
- Manage administrative needs such as documenting decisions, agreements, and results.

Second, determine if the people you are considering inviting will have decision-making authority *during* the meeting—either by default or by delegation. Delegated decision-making authority can work, as long as the ultimate decision maker will stand behind what his proxy committed to during the meeting.

And, third, before extending invitations, decide if it will be acceptable for invitees to send a representative, and if so, how the representative will *participate*. You don't want a room full of stand-ins there to take notes on what happens—you want everyone present to be *making* things happen.

These three steps ensure you are asking the right contributors to be there and positioning the meeting to accomplish its goals in the time allotted—rendering it anything but a waste of time.

>>> **Reality Check**: Are you currently inviting the usual suspects—with no forethought as to how they will contribute? Are you taking a good-things-come-in-small-packages approach—believing meetings should always be limited to some magical number of participants? Are you casting a wide net and inviting everyone to ensure no one is left out?

>>> **Bottom Line**: Determine who *needs* to attend based on how they will participate and what they will contribute in support of the meeting's purpose. Extend personal invitations to these people, sharing both the meeting's purpose and why they have been invited—to inspire them to accept your invitation. And then invite no one else.

PLANNER: Note-taking

Leading a meeting and recording during it are separate roles. Heed this powerful advice—do not attempt to simultaneously lead the meeting, chart comments made, and document decisions reached. Instead, enlist meeting members to chart content that should be on display in the meeting (a scribe) and to record the meeting's decisions and agreements (a recorder).

Here are some best practices to follow:

- Choose a *scribe* to chart working discussion notes. These will include brainstorming ideas to be voted on as the meeting progresses, options and alternatives identified during a problem-solving discussion, issues to be placed on a concerns chart (see more in Chapter 3), and so on.

- Choose a *recorder* to capture real-time meeting decisions. The document created will complement the scribe's work but will only include the meeting's findings and ultimate decisions, such as: the group's top-ranked ideas from the brainstormed list; their decision on which option(s) to pursue to resolve an issue; the issues requiring follow-up, who has ownership of each, deadlines for getting answers back to the group; and so on. The document will not record every comment made to arrive at the decisions. This guidance applies even when formal meeting minutes are required—with one difference. In meeting minutes, decisions will be aligned with motions made versus outcomes planned by the meeting leader—minutes are not a transcript.

- Pre-arrange with the scribe and recorder what their roles entail and what you need from each.

- Provide the scribe with two colors of markers and ask her to alternate colors for each new idea. In a virtual collaboration, ask her to change ink colors using the selected platform's tools.

- Provide the recorder with a summary of discussion template (see Tool 5-1 in Chapter 5) to streamline his recording efforts and create consistency from meeting to meeting.

- Direct the scribe's work during the meeting by telling her what to write down to capture the speaker's meaning and intent—succinctly.
- Periodically ask the recorder to read back what he has captured in his notes to ensure it is accurate, complete, and that everyone agrees with it.

>>> **Reality Check:** Do you believe everyone is taking the same notes of what has been agreed to during the meeting, what actions and deadlines others will be responsible for, and what actions and deadlines they will be responsible for after the meeting?

>>> **Bottom Line:** They aren't. And, if it isn't written down, it didn't happen. A results-driven meeting has one complete written account of its decisions and agreed-upon next steps that all in attendance acknowledge accurately represent the meeting. An engaging meeting drives active participation by capturing and displaying the group's work as they perform it. And a meeting in which people are inspired to follow through has both—without engagement there will be no results, and without results no one will be inspired.

PLANNER: Expectations

Expectations are multi-directional in meetings—you have expectations of participants and they hold expectations of you. Acting in accordance with those that you, as the meeting leader, will be held to will be critical to your success. Establishing—and communicating—yours for the participants will be too.

What Will Your Participants Expect of You?

As the leader of the meeting, your participants will reasonably expect you to:

- **Do your homework.** When you are leading a meeting, you have stepped into a leadership role—even if only for the next 45 minutes. People only want to be led by those who demonstrate their ability to lead, so be prepared, anticipate questions, be

knowledgeable on the topic, or invite the right resources who will
serve as knowledge sources.

- **Start on time.** This sage advice sounds obvious enough. Why
  then is it consistently violated? A common reason for delaying
  the start is not having everyone present. If you fall into that trap,
  it becomes a self-perpetuating cycle. When you start today's
  meeting late to accommodate late arrivals, those who were on
  time will plan to be late for your next meeting. Break that cycle
  with prompt starts. If you think that sounds great in theory but
  still wonder what to do if the key decision maker hasn't arrived
  yet, read the Expert Secret on starting and ending on time on the
  next page.

- **End on time.** This complement to the previous expectation is
  also consistently violated, largely for two reasons—meeting plan-
  ners frequently begin late and often set meeting durations arbi-
  trarily. Perhaps you read online that meetings shouldn't be longer
  than 15 or 30 minutes. Maybe you defaulted to a one-hour
  meeting rationalizing "that should be long enough." Ending on
  time requires setting the appropriate duration in the first place.
  And you can only do that by defining the process to achieve each
  meeting outcome and calculating the time each needs. If you are
  thinking that sounds great, but you'd already be doing that if
  you knew how to, read Expert Secret: Starting and Ending On
  Time—Every Time, and Chapter 2.

- **Adhere to time limits within the meeting.** The best way to end
  the meeting on time is to start and end each *section* of the meeting on time. This may require setting a timer on the table during
  "30-second introductions," asking the timekeeper to announce
  a 5-minute warning during small group work, or displaying a
  countdown timer in your slide deck during breaks and small
  group work.

- **Run an engaging meeting.** Who likes being bored? I recently
  read survey results indicating that 35 percent of people in
  status meetings consider them a waste of time. How would
  your employees characterize your staff meetings? Engagement
  counteracts boredom, and people engage when they are able to

Expert Secret:
Starting and Ending On Time—Every Time

Starting On Time

You want to start on time, you planned to start on time, but a glance around the room reveals a key decision maker hasn't arrived. Now what? Get started—because you planned for this! Whether there is a culture of tardiness in your environment, key individuals have well-earned reputations for arriving late, or life just happened to someone critical to your meeting, you need to anticipate late joiners and no-shows. Plan an opener that moves the group toward the goal of the meeting and also makes it easy for latecomers to engage when they arrive. Don't confuse this with "filler." You can, for example, set the desired climate with an appropriate story, lead introductions asking each person to share a strength they have that aligns with the meeting's goal, and so on. Another option—when you know participants will be late—is to connect with them beforehand, gather their input, and request permission to reiterate comments to the group if needed. This way, you can say something like "When Tim and I discussed this, he shared it would be critical that we consider . . .", or something similar and appropriate.

Ending On Time

If ending on time seems easier said than done and you are wondering how to do it, heed this direction and read all of Chapters 3 and 4.

The best way to know how much time meeting components will require—so you can then allocate the right time to each—is to begin paying attention to and tracking time in meetings you are invited to. Use your phone's stopwatch feature to note the time required for participant introductions, discussions, brainstorming, casting votes, or recapping meeting agreements. After the meetings, reflect on the times—were they sufficient, did they feel excessive and drawn out, or were they just about right? Then, use your heightened awareness and informed perspective to set timings when crafting your meeting agendas.

Chapters 3 and 4 will guide you in proactively and reactively corralling behaviors that can otherwise wreak havoc on your meeting's timeline.

contribute (see section on Names earlier in the chapter). Another powerful cure for boredom is having a role to perform (see Responsibilities later in this chapter).

- **Remain focused.** This almost seems contradictory: Participants want you to remain focused while they bring up tangents and hidden agendas! In essence, they want you to maintain control of the meeting—have a plan, stick to it, and get them to their next meeting on time. So, lean on your agenda—have one, share it, refer to it, and adhere to it.
- **Set up rules.** Social agreements—also known as ground rules or guidelines—go hand in hand with remaining focused and maintaining control. Participants want you to set boundaries so that everyone knows the rules and either adheres to them or is called into line for overstepping them.
- **Acknowledge their ideas.** People want to be heard, understood, and acknowledged—even when their ideas cannot be implemented. Charting performed by the scribe will be a powerful aid to recognizing people's input. Being able to see and refer back to ideas shared in the discussion formally recognizes them and gives them greater credence.

What Can You Expect of Your Participants?

Having expectations of meeting participants isn't sufficient. The expectations need to be *expressed*—and expressed clearly. They also need to be reiterated and reinforced. If you doubt that, read the scenario in the sidebar on the next page, and see if you recognize and can relate to the situation one senior vice president experienced—a situation faced by meeting leaders on a daily basis.

You can reasonably have the following expectations of your meeting participants—but only if you communicate them!

- **Arrive prepared.** People can amaze you with what they don't do. In their defense, have you clarified what arriving prepared will look like? Some examples of arriving prepared include having access to their calendars, having read the vendors' proposals, coming with a specific number of ideas for each agenda item, being ready to take notes (digital or paper based), or having

Great Expectations: One SVP's Story

A newly hired senior vice president called a staff meeting to update her team on revisions to a mission-critical standard operating procedure (SOP) affecting the group's work. A few weeks later, she confided her frustration with her staff to her executive coach: "I don't get this place! Two weeks ago, I brought the whole team together to share this update. No one wrote a thing down or even brought a pen and pad. No one asked any questions either—I'm not even sure they were listening to me. And then, this morning, one of them sent a group email saying the process that had been in place—the one I updated them on—no longer works and needs to be revised. To make matters worse, two staff replied in agreement saying they experienced the same thing. I feel like I might lose my mind."

In response, her coach asked a series of questions. Were the new work expectations specifically stated? "Well, no, but I literally told them how the SOP changed." Did you tell them the purpose of the meeting in advance and ask them to arrive prepared to take notes on how their duties would be shifting? "Should I need to tell professionals to bring a pad and pen to a meeting? And, being their boss, do I have to justify a reason for calling a meeting?" Did you send out a written summary of the meeting? "Well, no, but I told them all exactly how the SOP changed— and it seems no one put it together that I needed them to actually implement this change. Do I need to spoon-feed them everything?"

From the coach's perspective the disconnect was obvious: The team did not follow up on implementing the SOP because they weren't asked to. It is a story that plays out time and again. Like a formulaic movie script, the details change, but the story remains the same. If you are reliving this story like Bill Murray in *Groundhog Day*, break the pattern with the actions detailed in the Expectations component of PLANNER.

completed other pre-meeting actions you specified. If you don't specify these preparation expectations, don't be surprised when they don't happen.

- **Participate.** Meetings that lack participation can be awkward and uncomfortable—such as those characterized by the leader who asks a question and, when he gets no responses, quickly fills the void with "OK, well here is what I was thinking. . . ." At the opposite extreme, meetings in which participants dominate, ramble, negate everything, introduce tangents, or "participate" in other counterproductive ways can be as or even more painful to experience.

Yes, you want participation—but not all participation is created equally. If you expect people to automatically participate productively in response to "I'd like to have everyone's participation today," you will likely be disappointed. Instead, define what your desired participation for a given meeting looks like, communicate it to participants before the meeting, reiterate it at the meeting's start, and restate it as needed throughout. Desired participation will not be static—it will and should vary for different meetings, based on the outcomes. A few examples of shifting participation needs include the following: remaining open to alternative approaches, two ideas from each person on X, identifying a positive aspect of an idea prior to critiquing it, and so on.

- **Refrain from counterproductive behaviors.** Sure, we all want meeting participants to behave professionally and be productive contributors—even if the meeting is composed of volunteers or homeowners versus professional peers. How is it, then, that so many meetings are characterized by people who don't and aren't? Chapters 3 and 4 provide strategies to head off disruptive behavior and manage those disruptions that still surface. For now though, recognize you need to set the expectations to be able to hold meeting members accountable for them.
- **Seek and achieve clarity on post-meeting expectations.** Informational meetings, like the SVP's meeting in the sidebar, run the risk of becoming one-way data dumps if participants don't share the responsibility for reaching a common vision of what appropriate actions and behaviors following the meeting will look like. To process how newly acquired information will affect them and what will be expected of them going forward, people need to ask questions, answer questions, offer examples describing their interpretation of the new expectations, seek direction on how to handle anomalies that arise, and much more.

- **Take responsibility for post-meeting action items.** The reason you are meeting in the first place is for things to *happen*. Once decisions have been made in support of the goals, follow-through is required. In essence, for a meeting to be successful, everyone there needs to know who will do what and by when—and then do it! Attendance isn't the expectation; participation during the meeting and ownership of actions after the meeting are. Falling short of this renders an otherwise seemingly productive meeting useless.

>>> **Reality Check:** Did these expectations read like common sense to you? Are they behaviors that "everyone knows" are expected of them? Do you think people should do all of these things without being told to?

>>> **Bottom line:** Although you may not be wrong in answering yes to any of those questions, you would be wrong to believe that expected behaviors happen on their own. Meeting-fatigued individuals with competing demands for their time typically only rise to the standards explicitly required of them. If you don't express your expectations, don't be surprised when they are not met.

PLANNER: Responsibilities

On sports teams, even teams with only two players—as in beach volleyball, bobsledding, and tennis doubles—each person has a specific position, function, or role. These roles may be interchangeable—but they are always defined. Each team member knows what they are responsible for as well as what every other team member is tasked with. An effective meeting is no different. Here are common roles for effective meetings (notice that "seat warmer" isn't included!):

Leader

The leader convenes the meeting and is the primary point of communication before and after the meeting. The leader either plans, leads, and manages the meeting or enlists a facilitator to perform some or all of the planning, lead-ing, and meeting management. When the leader brings in a facilitator, she retains her leadership status, while freeing herself to participate as a contribu-tor instead of the leader.

Facilitator

When enlisted, the facilitator collaborates with the leader pre-meeting to determine the desired outcomes and the processes for achieving them. During the meeting, the facilitator clarifies roles, takes ownership of the process, manages group dynamics, coordinates the actions of the remaining roles, and takes ultimate responsibility for the meeting. This role does not contribute to the content of the meeting.

Scribe

The scribe creates a real-time visual display of the meeting's outputs. Typically, this is handwritten on a flip chart or smartboard. Variations include building a digital mind map of the discussion that is projected as it is being created or using whiteboard features of webinar software during virtual meetings. The scribe's work is visible to all *as it is being created.*

Recorder

Unlike the scribe, the recorder's work is not commonly displayed as devel-oped. A meeting should have both a scribe and a recorder. The scribe is akin to a cartographer, mapping the meeting so all can see where the group is and where it has been in support of getting where it wants to be, whereas the recorder documents the journey's final destination and next steps. The recorder creates the summary of discussion (Chapter 5) that documents information discovered, decisions agreed to, action items identified, and action items' deadlines and responsible individuals assigned, in addition to such logistics as attendance, time, date, location, and next meeting.

Timekeeper

There is more to this role than calling "time's up!" at the end of the meeting. The timekeeper will monitor and announce timings throughout the meeting, including 60-second introductions, 2-minute subgroup debriefs, a 5-minute guest speaker presentation, 8-minute brainstorming sessions, and so on. This role will take its timing cues from the facilitator or meeting leader.

Troubleshooter

Having an individual dedicated to dealing with the undesired and unexpected can make either less disruptive. Such distractions can include temperature fluctuations, audio visual failures, Internet connectivity issues, lighting, catering, interruptions at the door, misdirected calls coming in on a conference room phone, noise from adjoining spaces or facilities crews, dropped calls or software glitches during a virtual meeting, and more.

Contributors

Everyone in the meeting will have at least one defined role. If none of the previously listed roles applies to meeting participants, they should be there as active contributors. Identifying this role and specifically assigning it to meeting members is a proactive technique for obtaining the desired group participation.

Expert Secret:
The Devil Is in the Detail

Your attention to subtle details will set you apart in applying PLANNER. As you use the model, be sure to:

- ☐ Draft meeting outcomes so that large goals are broken down into their component parts. This lets you acknowledge progress more frequently during the meeting to maintain—or generate—momentum.
- ☐ Assign the same responsibilities to participants for a series of meetings to maintain consistency and streamline functions.
- ☐ Rotate responsibilities among participants for standing meetings to avoid complacency.

For more expert meeting secrets about planning your meetings, along with phrases you can integrate into your pre-meeting conversations and emails, check out www.KimberlyDevlin.com.

Other Roles

Based on the type and size of the meeting you are leading—such as open enrollment meetings, public hearings, or community outreach meetings—there may be additional roles to define and assign, such as guest presenter, registration desk coordinator, or greeters to guide guests to the room or assigned tables. You may even need a designated person to demonstrate a software system, navigate a website, or distribute materials during the meeting. Think through your meetings' needs and plan accordingly.

>>> **Reality Check:** Instead of leading the meeting, are you serving as its Sherpa—carrying the load of all these roles?

>>> **Bottom Line:** Sharing the load of a meeting's many responsibilities will minimize your burden as its leader, engage participants, increase accountability among all, lead to better results, generate ownership, and inspire people to follow your lead instead of criticize your need to exert control.

Tool 1-2: PLANNER Framework's Key Actions

This quick-reference job aid specifies the essential activities associated with each component of the PLANNER framework.

Purpose	Define clear meeting outcomes.
Location	Choose a meeting space that is convenient, neutral, and conducive to achieving your desired outcomes.
Agenda	Plan the activities or processes that support achieving the meeting's outcomes. (Chapter 2 is dedicated to agendas).
Names	Determine participants, your reason for inviting each, and their contributions to achieving the outcomes.
Note-taking	Clarify who will record decisions and action items during the meeting.
Expectations	Set expectations for all participants and integrate them into the meeting.
Responsibilities	Identify meeting roles and delegate responsibilities to all.

To Sum Up Planning Your Meeting

When a meeting runs well, finishes on time, accomplishes its goals, and concludes with a written summary of decisions and action items that everyone in attendance understands, agrees to, and has a role in supporting, it is because the meeting planner put thought, time, and effort into designing an effective event. The time you invest *before* your meeting to work through the PLANNER framework will pay off exponentially during and after your meeting. Use the strategies in the remaining chapters to complement and perpetuate your PLANNER efforts. Next up: agenda dos and don'ts.

Put It Into Practice

Your Action Items for Leading Meetings That Inspire, Engage, and Get Results

Earlier in this chapter, you were invited to record what you suspected goes into using PLANNER effectively (Tool 1-1). Now that you know the details behind PLANNER—and what you may have been overlooking—what do you need to do to get your meeting planning in shape? Use this worksheet to set your action plan as you refer to the PLANNER Framework's Key Actions job aid (Tool 1-2) and your notes on Tool 1-1.

PLANNER Framework	Actions to Improve My PLANNER Performance
Purpose	
Location	
Agenda	
Names	
Note-taking	
Expectations	
Responsibilities	

ONE-MINUTE
ROUNDUP

Planning for Success

Need this chapter's essence in a minute? Here it is:

GET RESULTS

- Never go into a meeting without knowing what you want to get out of it.
- Determine outcomes for every meeting by answering: "What does success look like?" and "What do I need to achieve with this meeting?"
- Be sure you can complete this statement *before* your meeting: "This meeting will be effective if we leave with _____."
- If it isn't written down . . . it didn't happen. Assign a recorder and guide him to record agreements reached and outcomes of discussions—*not* a record of everything said!

ENGAGE

- Have all of the right people present—and *only* the right people present.
- Communicate expectations before the meeting and reiterate them during the meeting.
- Prepare a well-crafted agenda to define for everyone what they are in the meeting to do and how they will collaborate to achieve it—this is a necessity for all meetings.
- Plan now, shine later—showing up 15 minutes before the scheduled meeting start time is *not* the equivalent of pre-planning.

INSPIRE

- Align participants' responsibilities in the meeting with their interests, strengths, and unique talents.
- Earn participants' confidence, respect, and support by getting the details right—be precise about location information, establish expectations and uphold them, ensure the right people are in the right meeting roles, and so on.
- Set realistic expectations for the meeting so that it is a success, as defined by accomplishing meaningful, tangible, or observable outcomes—getting results.

"Great things are not done by impulse,
but a series of small things brought together."
—Vincent Van Gogh

Find more at www.KimberlyDevlin.com.

What Belongs on the Agenda?

Seven Key Elements for Every Agenda

"If you do not know where you are going,
every road will get you nowhere."
—Henry Kissinger

A meeting without an agenda is like a road trip without a map. Is it possible you will take the most direct route and arrive at the desired destination? Sure, but neither ending is particularly likely. Equally true, if your map is outdated, covers the wrong area, or has too much or too little detail, you can expect a rough trip. The same pitfalls in your agenda will result in "don't waste my time" attitudes from participants in your meetings. As you prepare your agenda to get results, also build in elements that will inspire and engage. Plan for high levels of active participation and design an opening that establishes this expectation. Consider what decisions subcommittees can own versus what the full team must achieve consensus on. Dedicate the majority of time to group work when you have subcommittees. Anticipate meeting dynamics to decide what processes will be effective and received enthusiastically. And, determine how you will close the meeting to ensure post-meeting action.

These tips and the guidance in this chapter will help you whip your next agenda into shape—quickly and easily.

>>> **Reality Check:** Do you ever cite the following reasons for not preparing an agenda?

- It is a waste of paper.
- I don't have the time for that.
- I want to set an informal tone, and an agenda is too formal.

>>> **Bottom Line:** It is only a waste of paper if you fill it with useless content. Once you have planned your meeting using the PLANNER framework (see Chapter 1), building the agenda happens quickly. The agenda doesn't make a meeting formal—it makes it productive!

The Seven Elements for Every Agenda

There are seven key elements for every agenda: title, time, location, members, outcomes, agenda items, and next steps. But before we look at each element in more detail, let's take a moment to define what *should not* be on the agenda distributed to participants:

- ✗ A list of discussion topics
- ✗ Minute-by-minute timings
- ✗ A welcome message
- ✗ Mission and vision of the organization
- ✗ Names of everyone celebrating a birthday or work anniversary this month
- ✗ A questions and answers (Q&A) segment
- ✗ Exhibits, reference materials, and so on
- ✗ Anything that pushes the agenda beyond one page—in most instances

A well-crafted agenda establishes your objectives, drives the meeting's processes, and keeps the meeting on track. A bulleted list of discussion topics supports none of that. Minute-by-minute timings will actually direct

Expert Secret: Pre-Game Hype

What do weddings, concerts, and football games have in common? They all leverage pre-game hype—save-the-date announcements are sent, local radio stations play the artist's music the week before, tailgate parties precede the event. For your meeting, creating an effective agenda is only one part of the equation for success. Your well-crafted agenda also should be shared before the meeting—though admittedly pre-meeting hype will be lower key than celebration, performance, or sport hype—and adhered to during the meeting. The following phrases can be useful in emails conveying the agenda before your event:

☐ "To ensure productive use of your time, I prepared the attached agenda that outlines our goals and processes for the meeting."

☐ "Please arrive prepared to contribute by: [specify required actions as bullet points]."

☐ "This meeting will be held at [location]; please allow additional travel time due to [specify, such as: road construction in the area, limited parking, enhanced security screening, and so on, as applicable]."

☐ "This meeting is being hosted over [platform]; please download the software in advance and dial-in early to check your connection."

For additional phrases you can use during the meeting, check out www.KimberlyDevlin.com. You can also find the *Meeting Expert's Toolkit Bundle* there that includes a checklist of action items for creating effective agendas.

attention away from what the team is there to accomplish and toward monitoring whether the meeting has fallen behind schedule. The remaining items on that list may have a place in the overall meeting experience—such as in an agenda transmission email, on a visual used in the meeting, as elements of the meeting processes, or as resources distributed prior to or during the meeting—but not on the agenda.

Meeting Title, Time, and Location: Basic But Often Overlooked

Let's begin with three key elements that are simple to include and easy to get wrong: meeting title, time, and location.

> *"I don't know why they call it common sense;*
> *it isn't all that common."*
> —Regina Devlin (my grandmother)

Meeting Title

In a few words, label the event. Be descriptive, be distinctive, and keep it simple.

Descriptive, in this context, means the title should convey meaning to the participants—is this a kickoff meeting, a leadership retreat, a planning meeting, a debriefing session? Determine what type of meeting it is and include that in the title.

Distinctive refers to providing a unique name for the meeting that distinguishes it from every other meeting this group attends together. For example, working with a cross-representational steering committee to plan a large-scale community visioning process, we knew there would be many meetings leading up to the full-day forum event. Vision 20xx Planning Meeting #1, Vision 20xx Planning Meeting #2, and so on were used to name the seven meetings that led to the event. Even recurring team meetings will benefit from this strategy, but instead of just numbering them, consider other options:

- Week 1, Week 2, . . . Week 51, Week 52
- January, February, March . . .
- Q1, Q2, Q3, Q4
- Winter, Spring, Summer, Fall

The importance of keeping it simple can also been seen in the example above. Because "Vision 20xx" was the committee's selected name for the forum, using it in the title put the meeting into the participants' context (versus "City of Wilkerson Project," which would have been our context as external consultants). Adding "planning meeting" to the title described its purpose in just a few words, and the addition of a number provided distinction without adding complexity.

Time

An error in this part of your agenda can wreak havoc on your meeting. Avoid typos that will lead to confusion by using the day/date/time structure. I recently received an email requesting my availability on Thursday, November 16. Consulting my calendar, I saw the 16th was a Friday and asked for clarification—in reality, the invitation was intended for Thursday, December 6—quite a discrepancy! When you specify both the day of the week and the date of the month, scheduling errors are more likely to be noticed and questioned—and therefore fixed, when needed.

Follow the day/date information with both the start and end times. If you have ever seen people stand up mid-meeting and say "I assumed we would be finished by now and am scheduled for another meeting" as they walk out, you know the importance of defining meeting end times.

You can also prevent 12-hour clock system confusion by including a.m. or p.m. beside the times. This is especially true for meetings of shift workers, in 24x7 work environments, with meetings of community-based groups (such as homeowners, civic groups, or school committees), or industry/professional associations that may be meeting outside of common business hours. Lastly, specifying the time zone will also be key when your meetings occur virtually and participants are geographically dispersed.

Location

For your face-to-face meetings, remember that when you are familiar with a place, it is easy to overlook that others may not be. Therefore, make it easy on everyone—include both the building name and the street address, and specify the room number and room name if it has both. Some rooms have functional names (main conference room, board room, IT lab), or assigned names (302B, 515), but many meeting spaces have nicknames (downtown, the tower, the dungeon, the mezzanine, and the like). How is the room known and how will it most easily be found? Head off disconnects by providing all the location data the participants will need.

Not all meetings take place face to face though. Should you still include "location" on the agenda for virtual meetings and those occurring over a phone line? Yes—it avoids confusion, clarifies expectations, and maintains a consistent agenda format. Simply indicate "Virtual meeting via GoToMeeting" or the selected platform, or "Via conference call bridge" followed by the call-in number.

Now that you've had a taste of some of the components of effective agendas, look over Seven Secrets for Agendas That Work (Tool 2-1). It shows how the first three elements work together in a sample agenda. It also gives you a look ahead to the other four components of effective agendas.

Tool 2-1: Seven Secrets for Agendas That Work

Can such commonsense stuff be considered secrets? Yes! Because so few people actually include these components when crafting their agendas—if they use an agenda at all. Study this sample agenda and use it as a reference when preparing yours. To save time, download the digital versions of the agenda template, part of the *Meeting Expert's Toolkit Bundle*, at www.KimberlyDevlin.com.

Agenda Components	Sample Content	
Meeting Title	Vision 20xx Steering Committee Planning Meeting #2	
Day/Date Time	Friday, November 26, 20xx 6:00-8:00 p.m.	
Location	City's Tennis Center (room 4B) 420 W. State Street	
Meeting Members	— Ronnie Glotzbach	EdTrek facilitator
	— Kimberly Devlin	EdTrek recorder
	— Kevin Vee	City liaison
	— Maria Hernandez	Steering Committee
	— Victor Marks	Steering Committee
	— Armando Stiles	Steering Committee
	— Sue Waltrip	Steering Committee
	— Hector Washington	Steering Committee
Meeting Outcomes	• Agreement on Steering Committee responsibilities • Brand for Vision 20xx • Attendee profile and criteria defined • Invitation process defined and instrument drafted • Next steps defined (remaining key actions for Forum success)	

Agenda Items	(what)	(how)	(who)	(time)
	Roles and responsibilities	Facilitated conversation	All	6:00–6:15 15 min.
	Brand . . . Attendee profile . . . Invitation process . . .	Concurrent breakout groups	Steering Comm.	6:15–7:30 75 min.
		Report-outs	Breakout group repre- sentatives	7:30–7:45 15 min.
	Next Steps	Facilitated conversation	All	7:45–8:00 15 min.
Next Steps	— Meeting #3: Forum agenda planning (12/10/20xx) — Meeting #4: Outcomes TBD (Date TBD) — Post-forum meeting: Debrief event, share feedback on draft vision statement (Date TBD)			

Members: What Is the Best Way to List Meeting Participants?

The fourth critical component of your agenda will be who is attending. Back in Chapter 1, the Names component of PLANNER walked you through how to identify who to include in your meeting. Now, you have a few options for identifying each person on the agenda. Here are two to avoid: skipping names and simply labeling the group—such as ABC Project Team, department staff, or sales force—or just listing names with nothing more.

Instead, consider which identifiers—title, department/organization, function, or some hybrid of these—is best suited to your event and your goals for it. (The sample agenda in Tool 2-1 follows a hybrid approach.) Here are some questions to guide your choice:

- Do the meeting members already know one another?
- Do you want to leverage or downplay position-based seniority?
- Will egos play a significant role in this meeting?
- Is everyone from the same organization?
- What information do meeting members need to interact most effectively?
- How will participants want to see themselves listed?

By Title

Perhaps the most common practice, indicating titles beside participants' names will likely encourage participants to defer to the most senior individuals. To counteract that tendency—if it will not offend the highest-ranking participants—list names alphabetically instead of by seniority.

By Department or Organization

Grouping names under department or organization headings can help participants see the big picture behind participants' perspectives, suggestions, personal agendas, as well as authority and responsibility during the meeting and after it.

By Function in Relation to the Project

Not only will this approach inform everyone of each person's role, it can also send each person a polite message of how they are expected to participate. Consider a task force committee composed of directors and senior executives from multiple organizations—people used to being in charge. Assigning them all the same role of "committee member," after specifying one name as "committee chair" and another as "committee vice chair," communicates their redefined status in this group.

Expert Secret: One Meeting, Two Agendas

Many things that can and do go wrong in meetings can be traced to a poorly crafted agenda. Your meetings need well-crafted agendas. In fact, you may want two: one for meeting members and another that you will work from as the meeting leader or facilitator. The difference between the two will be their levels of detail. Providing a streamlined one-page agenda to participants will guide everyone through the meeting's processes seamlessly. Your expanded leader's agenda, however, may include more detail such as timing breakdowns for each agenda item's process, notes to refer to, or quotes or statistics you intend to share. Having these in your copy of the agenda will help you keep the meeting on schedule, on task, and productive.

The Meeting Participants' Agenda

Your meeting members' agenda will provide participants with all of the following:

- What meeting has been scheduled
- How much time to block
- Where they will be meeting
- Who else is attending
- What each person's contributions to the meeting will be
- The meeting's purpose
- The meeting's processes
- How much time is dedicated to each agenda item
- What may be expected after the meeting

How does this list compare to the last agenda you prepared? Or received?

The Meeting Leader's Agenda

Your detailed version will support you—or your facilitator if you have one—in running the meeting by providing the following:

- A tool to easily track present and absent invitees (add checkboxes beside participants' names to facilitate this).
- A bird's-eye view of the meeting's planned flow (include detailed versions of what, how, who, and when).
- A quick reference guide to timing breakdowns (such as the individual time allocations for brainstorming, prioritizing options, and reaching consensus within a 35-minute agenda item).
- Details that support agenda items (for example, if "agreement on committee member roles" is an outcome, your leader's agenda could include a list of the expectations of each role to refer to during the meeting).
- An outline of talking points associated with each agenda item (to keep you focused and ensure everything intended to be addressed is covered).

Your well-crafted agenda will be a powerful tool that prepares participants, supports you, and keeps the meeting focused and productive.

Meeting Outcomes, Not Discussion Items

When your agenda mistakenly lists discussion topics instead of outcomes, it is hard—if not impossible—for anyone to know what they are there to *achieve*. Little or nothing is accomplished, and the perception of an effective meeting as a mythical creature is reinforced once more. Break that cycle with your diligent integration of the fifth agenda component, outcomes.

Your meeting outcomes come directly from your PLANNER efforts (refer back to Purpose in Chapter 1). They are the tangible or observable results you are meeting to achieve. Outcomes answer the why-are-we-meeting question for all participants—including you as the meeting's leader.

>>> **Reality Check:** Does it seem that a list of discussion topics is sufficient and that exerting effort to craft outcomes is a waste of your time?

>>> **Bottom Line:** In a study conducted for *Harvard Business Review,* more than 75 percent of participants said they were annoyed by meetings they deem unnecessary. If people don't know why they are meeting, how can they see your meeting as necessary? If they deem your meeting unnecessary, how can you hope to inspire them, engage them, or get results? So, define your meeting's goals and then share the outcomes to demonstrate that your meeting won't waste their time.

Agenda Items: If I Have Meeting Outcomes, Why Do I Need Agenda Items?

> *"The only way around is through."*
> —Robert Frost

The sixth agenda component, agenda items, drives the meeting's processes. In the spirit of the Robert Frost quote above, your agenda items lay out your path "through" the meeting. Outcomes are your *goals,* whereas agenda items are the *processes* for achieving them. The two elements are directly related—but are not the same. Without agenda items, there is no strategy in place for accomplishing the outcomes. And meetings that inspire, engage, and get results always have a defined strategy.

>>> **Reality Check:** Feeling a little confused over outcomes and agenda items?

>>> **Bottom Line:** Meeting outcomes are *what* you will achieve. Agenda items are *how* you will achieve them.

Do I expect your agenda item processes to include discussions? You bet I do. Be sure to include other processes or techniques as well to engage everyone, enhance the meeting's pace, and generate enthusiasm. Here are some to consider: individual brainwriting followed by a round-robin of ideas, traditional brainstorming, subgroup work, brief presentations, nominal group technique, multi-voting, and other facilitation methods. I have assembled a few tools to get you started if these processes are new to you—you can find them in the *Meeting Expert's Toolkit Bundle* at www.KimberlyDevlin.com.

One technique to avoid in most instances is Q&A. The reason you were advised, earlier, to leave Q&A segments off of your agenda is that questions and their answers should typically surface throughout the meeting—within the processes you plan. You will want to engage participants throughout instead of holding their involvement until you have finished boring them!

Next Steps: What Happens Now?

The seventh agenda component, next steps, ensures everyone is looking ahead—beyond the meeting's end time. That may be to the next time the group convenes, to their follow-through on action items, or both.

In the case of stand-alone meetings, your agenda can simply list next steps as a meeting element and allocate time to it. When you reach this point in the meeting, review and assign action items, set deadlines, and—as a savvy meeting leader—ask each person to reiterate their understanding of what they are doing and by when. Also reach agreement on how the group will follow up on their follow-through (for more on this, see Chapter 5). Will software or an app such as Teamwork or Trello be used to show completion?

Will each person email status updates to the group? Will a different follow-up process be implemented?

For ongoing project or task meetings, you want to be more prescriptive about next steps on your agenda. Inspire and engage the group by forecasting where the group is headed—list when the next few meetings are scheduled, succinctly specify what they will focus on. By planning the meeting dates and themes in advance, scheduling becomes easier, participants can see the bigger picture, and they develop confidence that you see it too. When you reach next steps during the meeting, perform the same actions previously described for stand-alone meetings to ensure you get results. Also confirm upcoming meetings' dates and times as well as participants' continued intent to participate; revise the planned focus of those meetings if needed based on your progress to date; determine if additional working meetings are needed to achieve the project deliverables by the project deadline; and so on.

To Sum Up Agendas

Agendas establish your objectives, they drive the processes, they keep the meeting on track, and they signal to everyone involved that they can trust you to run a prepared and effective meeting—in other words—that you aren't going to waste their time!

"For every minute spent organizing, an hour is earned."
—Benjamin Franklin

Put It Into Practice

Apply PLANNER to Your Next Meeting

You discovered the PLANNER framework for creating and leading effective meetings in Chapter 1. In this chapter, you explored detailed agenda guidance on what to include on your agenda. Now put what you've learned to work for an upcoming meeting. Complete this PLANNER tool and then draft your agenda using the worksheet provided.

Upcoming Meeting:	
Purpose	
Location	
Agenda	*Use the detailed Agenda Worksheet on the next page for this PLANNER component.*
Names	
Note-taking	
Expectations	
Responsibilities	

Put It Into Practice

Create an Agenda for Your Next Meeting

Draw on your PLANNER to create your agenda for the same meeting.

Meeting Title:
Day/Date and Time:
Location:
Meeting Members:

Meeting Outcomes:

Agenda Items:

(what)	(how)	(who)	(time)
Opener			
Outcome #1			
Outcome #2			
Outcome #3			

Next Steps:

Agendas

Need this chapter's essence in a minute? Here it is:

GET RESULTS

- Build an agenda for every meeting.
- Replace a list of discussion topics on your agenda with meeting outcomes.
- Ensure your outcomes (*what* you will achieve) are phrased as tangible or observable results.
- Double-check the agenda's time and location details to avoid disconnects.
- Include next steps to maintain everyone's focus on what will happen next and by when.

ENGAGE

- List meeting members in the way most conducive to your meeting dynamics and your desired meeting outcomes—by title, department/organization, function, or a hybrid of these.
- Plan agenda items (*how* you will achieve your outcomes) using processes and techniques that involve the team.
- Assign responsibility for agenda items to multiple meeting participants.
- Seek meeting members' input on your agenda before the meeting to gain buy-in.

INSPIRE

- Set realistic timelines for agenda items so they can be completed in the allotted time.
- Vary agenda items' processes to prevent boredom and predictability.

- Have an agenda, stick to it, and accomplish what you set out to—and people will be inspired to attend your meetings!

"The beginning is the most important part of the work."
—Plato

Find more at www.KimberlyDevlin.com.

3

How Do I Prevent Bad Behavior Before It Begins?

50+ Proactive Strategies to Avoid Meeting Meltdowns

"The man who moves a mountain begins
by carrying away small stones."
—Confucius

The list of dreaded meeting meltdown scenarios is long. People can be complacent, argumentative, withdrawn, domineering, and negative; hidden agendas surface; turf wars break out; side conversations occur; discussions go on tangents; decisions made are revisited, questioned, or challenged; and counter-productive behaviors, such as disengaging, daydreaming, checking mobile devices, or sleeping (yes, I said it—and have seen it) are displayed.

When it comes to meeting behavior, we can follow the lead of toddlers' parents, who seem to know a universal truth: The easiest way to manage a meltdown is to prevent it before it begins. Creative parents pack and deploy a "magic bag" of toys, treats, and solutions; you can develop your own magic bag of techniques pulling from three categories: seating arrangements, charts, and openings.

Leveraging all three proactive categories will exponentially reduce the headaches you need to manage reactively (see Chapter 4 for strategies to manage the situations that slip through). They will also help your meetings be more engaging and comfortable for your participants.

Seating Strategies: What Emily Post Never Told You About Seating Arrangements

Although Ms. Post may be your go-to for social etiquette on how to seat solo guests, feuding family members, and officials at receptions, you need different guidance for your meetings. Here it is.

Expert Secret:
Proactive Behavior Management

The easiest challenges to resolve are the ones you prevent. Get ahead of disruptions with these actions that complement this chapter's strategies:

- Send an email a few days before a virtual meeting that includes this message: "This meeting is being hosted over [platform]; please download the software in advance and dial in early to check your connection."
- Warmly welcome individual members upon their arrival—begin building positive relationships immediately.
- Guide seat selection subtly by removing chairs, turning chairs to face a wall, or placing participant materials at the few seats where you want people to sit. As they arrive, invite them to sit anywhere they see materials set out. And, when you see someone take a set of materials and begin moving a chair, try: "Oh, we won't be using those tables today," or "I actually put those there for a reason—please take any of these open seats."
- Confirm the scheduled meeting duration when you begin and check that each person is still committed to participating in the full meeting.

For additional strategies and language you can use to proactively keep your meetings on track, check out the free bonus content at www.KimberlyDevlin.com.

When left to select their own seats (that is, open seating), people will typically choose based on factors that support their agendas, not yours. Examples include participants sitting far from you to avoid participating, sitting near an outlet to have uninterrupted power for their devices, and sitting by a door to be able to step out easily. Orchestrating seating proactively minimizes behavior issues by separating cliques and confrontational personalities, positioning people to engage instead of hide, subtly establishing your authority in the meeting as its leader, and making interventions easier to implement (Chapter 4).

Does this mean assigned seating is the solution? The answer is "maybe." Below are four seating options—random, partial random, targeted positioning, and selective positioning—with examples of how to use them and when they can serve you best. You might begin your meeting with one of these seating strategies or—more likely—ask participants to move as needed during the meeting.

Random Seating

Random seating is not the same as open seating. Open seating is the come-in-and-grab-the-seat-that-best-suits-your-agenda approach described above. With random seating, where each person sits will be arbitrary. As you saw, very little was arbitrary in the open seating examples above—in fact, people may even be predictable in their open seating choices. Random seating leads to engaged participants by getting people focused on your agenda instead of theirs.

Consider using random seating when:

- Meeting members are open-minded, willing, and eager participants.
- The meeting's pace is slowing, and standing to move to a new seat will provide a needed infusion of energy to the group.
- Participants are getting stuck on views, and a fresh perspective is needed.
- Meeting participants default to sitting in cliques.

How can you achieve random seating without incurring the downfalls inherent in open seating? Here are five ways to get your thinking started:

- **Order of Arrival.** Direct participants to fill seats at the same table until that table is full, then fill the next table, and so on.
- **Playing Cards.** Each member is given a playing card and sits accordingly. Consider these variations: find four of a kind and sit together, create a full house, sit at the table that matches your card's suit (label the tables), sit in numerical order around a conference table, and so on.
- **Color Code.** Color—in the form of stickers, marker ink, sticky notes, agenda paper, cardstock used for name tents, and so on— can be used to group people.
- **Categories.** Here, you are limited only by your imagination. For example, you can ask everyone to sit around the conference table in chronological order of their birthdays, based on the distance of their daily commutes, how far they traveled to get to the meeting, how many cups of caffeine they drank today, and so on.
- **Count Off.** Probably the most commonly used technique, counting off requires little planning and no support materials.

Partial Random Seating

With partial random, you set parameters for seat selection and allow individuals to choose their own seats—as long as the stated requirements are met. It is critical to set a time limit when using this approach. Try this: "You have 30 seconds to find a new seat; it must be a different seat than the one you are in now and you must have new elbow-mates." Giving meeting members an element of control over their seats can inspire them to contribute constructively.

Consider using partial random seating when you want to:

- Give participants an element of control over their seating
- Mix intact work groups
- Infuse energy (when parameters require an element of novelty)
- Generate discussion (when parameters require learning new information about one another).

Here are a few sample constraints to inspire your choice of parameters:

- Sit beside a person not from your department.
- Find a person you don't know and sit together.

- Everyone at your new table will have the same color somewhere in their outfit.
- Sit with a department peer with whom you don't frequently collaborate.
- Find a partner with whom you share an interest.

You can also use some of the same techniques previously listed for random seating, but in different ways to achieve partial random seating. Consider these examples:

- **Color Code.** The same devices—stickers, ink, sticky notes, agenda paper, and name tent cardstock—can be used to create parameters. In a meeting with four tables, for example, assign each table the same color initially; the parameter is that new groups cannot include anyone with the same color as yours. Or, at a conference room table, position tent cards of the same color beside one another and set the parameter for new seats as requiring other colors to your left and right.
- **Categories.** Again, it isn't the device, but how you use it that creates a partial random outcome. Examples for categories include sitting with a person who works for a different supervisor or a person who shares your preference for either printed books, e-books, audio books, or waiting for the movie. You might even select categories based on information you already know about the participants, such as languages spoken, union affiliation, first-time volunteers, number of direct reports, duration of service to the organization, and so on.

Targeted Positioning Seating

The targeted positioning strategy achieves seating arrangements with specific categories of individuals at each table or in each area of the room. It is "assigned" seating—except when it isn't. Targeted positioning *isn't* assigned seating when you pre-arrange groupings but allow groups to choose their tables and group members to choose their specific seats. It also *isn't* assigned seating when you plan the desired categories for the groups but determine their membership on the spot during the meeting. Targeted positioning *is* assigned seating when you pre-plan the groupings and set out place cards.

Whichever approach you follow, advance planning is the key to targeted positioning seating. This seating arrangement heavily supports getting results because people are carefully situated to achieve specific goals—whether those are meeting outcomes or underlying objectives such as relationship building, cross-pollenating of ideas, and so on.

Consider using targeted positioning seating when you want:

- Specific pairings in the groupings
- To align individuals' strengths with their subgroup work assignments
- To prevent power struggles in subgroups or challenging behaviors due to conflicting personalities being partnered
- To forge relationships between disparate parties.

Here are a few ways to achieve targeted positioning seating:

- **Pre-Planned Groupings.** Pre-plan your groups when the specific individuals in each group matters, your group is large, balancing the groups may be complicated, or meeting time will be at a premium. Next, determine the method you will use to introduce the groups, which could include options such as these:
  - Verbal announcement. Limit this approach to meetings of smaller groups.
  - Display groupings on a slide or flip chart. List names alphabetically—to ease locating one's name—and consider showing each group in a unique color—to ease moving into the groups.
  - Place cards. If you prepare the room with place cards set out, don't be surprised when early arrivals move their names after seeing who they are with or where they have been placed. Plan to be in the room early and intercept such behavior.
- **Group by Category and Pair Off.** To have predetermined traits represented in each pair, trio, or group, direct the meeting members to form multiple lines—such as teachers in one line, parents in a second, and students in a third—and then form trios with one person from each line.

Selective Positioning Seating

Selective positioning seating is the secret weapon of savvy meeting leaders. What makes it so powerful is that it *looks* random but is actually highly prescribed. Draw on it to manage negative dynamics you anticipate or see developing and when enhancing the group's productivity requires repositioning certain people but it would be inappropriate to call them out. This powerhouse strategy will influence your ability to inspire, engage, and get results by tackling multiple group needs simultaneously and doing it so cleverly that participants will be amazed at what impediments *didn't* surface during the meeting.

Consider using selective positioning seating when you need to achieve one or more of the following:

- Reposition a domineering person
- Reposition a withdrawn person
- Break up a subgroup that engages in side conversations
- Separate personalities
- Bring together select people without drawing attention to the move
- Accommodate a participant's disability
- Achieve any other specific seating arrangement without calling attention to it.

Here are a few ways to achieve this powerful seating strategy:

- **Playing Cards.** Each person is provided with a playing card and tables are labeled by suit or face values. Once everyone has a card, ask them to sit at the table that matches their card. So far, this sounds a lot like random seating—and it is, until you distribute cards strategically—even if only a handful of cards are purposefully distributed, so you know where those individuals will be sitting, and the rest are randomly passed out.
- **Color Code.** Follow the same approach as described above for playing cards but distribute multiple colors of index cards, sticky notes, blocks, candies, or anything else you choose to use. Again, there may only be select individuals whose color assignments matter—the rest can be random.

- **Count Off and Rotate Tables.** Everyone begins already seated at tables in any order. If you have four tables, participants will count off from zero to three; if you have six tables, from zero to five; and so on. To find their new seats, "zeros" remain in their seats, "ones" rotate clockwise to one table away, "twos" rotate clockwise to two tables away, and so on. You can use this technique to simply break up a rowdy table or to manage multiple seating needs at once. For example, to keep a nursing mom close to the door, bring an unengaged team member to the front of the room, and move a dominant personality to a less commanding position in the room, predetermine where you need those three people to end up and ensure your "random-looking" count-off gives them the numbers that will result in the positions you want for them.

>>> **Reality Check:** Do you quietly sigh, roll your eyes, or break into a mild sweat when people enter the meeting room and choose a seat that you know will lead to behavior challenges?

>>> **Bottom Line:** As meeting leader—lead it. Determine the seating that best achieves your goals, minimizes disruptive conduct, and engages participants—and then integrate it into your plan.

Put It Into Practice

Getting Ahead of Bad Behavior With Seating

In Chapter 2, you outlined your PLANNER and drafted an agenda for an upcoming meeting. With that meeting in mind, use this tool to choose and plan your preferred seating strategy for each agenda item.

Seating Options

Seating	Rationale for Using This Configuration	For These Agenda Items
Random	❐ Participants are likely to be open-minded, willing, and eager. ❐ Participants are likely to sit in cliques. ❐ Pace may be slowing and moving seats will infuse energy. ❐ Participants may be getting stuck and need a fresh perspective.	
Partial Random	❐ To give participants an element of control over their seating. ❐ To mix intact work groups. ❐ To infuse energy (include novelty in the parameters). ❐ To generate discussion (include discovery in the parameters).	
Targeted Positioning	❐ Specific pairings are needed in the groupings. ❐ Individuals' strengths need to align with subgroup work. ❐ Power struggles could otherwise surface in subgroups. ❐ Conflicting personalities could otherwise derail subgroups. ❐ Relationship building is needed.	

Continued on next page

Seating	Rationale for Using This Configuration	For These Agenda Items
Selective Positioning	❐ Dominant personalities may need to be repositioned. ❐ Withdrawn people may need to be repositioned. ❐ Sidebar conversations may be likely. ❐ Opposing personalities may be present. ❐ Select people need to be brought together—or separated—without drawing attention to the move. ❐ Disabilities may need to be accommodated. ❐ Another specific arrangement is needed without bringing attention to it.	

Charts: Charting a Course to Better Behavior

Your proactive strategies for managing participant behaviors must include strategic use of charting. A few simple wall charts will take little effort to create but will prompt appropriate participation, manage the off topic, and track your progress. Specifically, you will want charts for guidelines, concerns, and agreements. If you lead meetings without these tools, you will be working harder than needed and your effectiveness quotient will plummet. Take the guidance below to heart—and to your next meeting.

Guidelines Chart (aka Social Agreements or Ground Rules)

This chart—prominently displayed and ideally referred to early in the meeting—establishes boundaries that will lead to a successful meeting. Boundaries can include voicing concerns constructively, allowing everyone to be heard, soliciting opposing views, and remaining open minded, as well as basics such as setting devices to meeting mode and adhering to time limits.

When and how you create this chart can vary. By prerecording all the guidelines, you will save time but will also convey a strong I-am-in-charge message. Maybe that is OK—maybe it isn't. To increase engagement and gain more participant buy-in, you may prefer to only prerecord the must-have guidelines and allow the group to set the additional participation boundaries at the start of the meeting. When participant ownership of the process is a priority, however, your best option may be to have the group generate the complete list. Often, they will draw a harder line than you would have.

However you choose to develop your guidelines, displaying them on a chart will focus attention on appropriate behavior throughout the meeting. It will also increase peer accountability, enabling anyone to refer to it should participants overstep or tread closely to a boundary.

Concerns Chart (aka Parking Lot)

Your concerns chart is a respectful placeholder for anything that surfaces that is off topic, outside of the group's control, or tangentially related but not on the agenda.

It is not enough to record items on a concerns chart. You need to acknowledge them as well. When closing the meeting, refer back to the concerns chart and—as fits each item—include them on a subsequent agenda, delegate action on them to meeting members, locate answers to those that are questions, or tactfully refer select items back to the people who mentioned them, and so on. By capturing participants' concerns—and returning to them to determine associated next steps—your meeting participants will feel valued and heard, engage more fully in your agenda, and admire your meeting leadership style. Meanwhile, you will accomplish what you set out to—and those achievements will be captured on your third chart.

Agreements Chart (aka Decisions Chart)

This chart—prominently displayed and built upon throughout the meeting—records the group's decisions in real time as they are made. As such, it prevents confusion, avoids misunderstandings, and updates anyone who stepped out of the meeting—physically or mentally. At the beginning of your meeting, display the pre-labeled chart and explain how it will be used to track decisions.

Your agreements chart will inspire participants by highlighting what *has been* accomplished. It will engage—or reengage—participants who disconnect. And, it will ensure your meeting gets results by preventing the group from circling back to agenda items that already have closure.

>>> **Reality Check:** Think flip charts and whiteboards are only used in training events, to map processes, or to provide Wi-Fi information to groups using a meeting room?

>>> **Bottom Line:** Recording and displaying guidelines, concerns, and agreements on wall charts emphasizes them during your meeting, gives you greater facilitative control of the event, and provides visual and physical reference points you can return to if challenges arise. They are easy to use and foolish to overlook.

 Put It Into Practice

Staying Ahead of Bad Behavior With Charts

You used the last worksheet to get ahead of bad behaviors with seating. Plan to stay ahead of such behaviors by strategizing how you will leverage charts in your meeting.

Guidelines Chart

I will:

- ☐ Prepare it in advance and introduce the boundaries to the group.
- ☐ Pre-chart the "must haves" and invite the group to define additional boundaries.
- ☐ Facilitate the team's development of all the social agreements.

Must-have Guidelines for This Meeting:

Other Charts

Decide where you will display your agreements and concerns charts. By their nature, you cannot complete these in advance, but you can prepare them and choose suitable locations to display them. Keep your agreements chart front and center. Your concerns chart can be off to the side or potentially even in the back or hung on an exit door.

Openings: You Never Get a Second Chance to Make a First Impression

People are time-pressed. They are meeting weary. So, shouldn't you save everyone some time, forgo introductions, and get right to the business at hand? Unequivocally—no. If you do, you are giving up the opportunity to set a tone, subtly establish your expectation for participation from all, learn information you can use throughout the group's working relationship, and make clear that your meeting leadership style is facilitative and not dictatorial. Granted, none of these things will happen if your version of introductions is for each person in turn to recite their name and title.

For this section, we will look at three categories of meetings, each requiring a different approach to openings. First, we will address the bad news meeting—where you have been given the unenviable role of messenger. Second, we will consider ongoing meetings of teams, and, third, we will tackle new meetings of people coming together for the first time. All three require forethought and planning.

Don't Kill the Messenger: Delivering Bad News

Perhaps one of the most difficult meetings to lead is one in which you will be delivering disappointing news—layoffs, benefit changes, increased fees, budget cuts, and the like. Taking a rip-the-bandage-off-quickly approach is common, and these meetings often open with the words: "I have some bad news to share." Avoid that. Also avoid stalling tactics such as asking everyone to introduce themselves—that is not why this meeting is being held. Bad news meetings require a unique series of opening actions to head off a mutiny—here it is.

Use an opener that will create a neutral climate. This may be a story, a statistic, or a well-chosen quote. Consider, for example, this Chinese proverb: "The best time to plant a tree is 20 years ago—the second-best time is today." It acknowledges your recognition that the current situation is far from ideal and that you are asking the group to make the best of the situation with you.

From here, share the history of the situation. Succinctly provide an appropriate level of detail to answer: How did we arrive here? What happened? Who was involved? Why did this happen? By doing this, you are essentially covering all the questions the group will have initially. Only after opening and sharing the history will you have prepared the group for the bad news.

Now is the time to rip the bandage off quickly, so to speak. State the bad news concisely and move directly to presenting the alternatives people can choose from. Finally, you will use the rest of the meeting to guide the group to choose the preferred option.

Riding the Merry-Go-Round: Ongoing Meetings of Teams

Monthly staff meetings, project huddle meetings, board meetings, quarterly sales meetings—any meeting of a group that comes together periodically—will benefit from opening with introductions. The right introductions can add levity, increase awareness of fellow members, strengthen interpersonal relationships, offer surprising insight into where people are coming from, and create a space for rigorous honesty—all of which are critical if you want a group of people to be inspired, engaged, and achieve something together.

Clearly, I am not talking about "Hi, my name is [insert name here] and I am a [insert title here]." Instead, change up the information each person shares and how they share it from meeting to meeting. I rely on four categories of introductions: intriguing questions, superlatives, novelty, and perceptions. See the Expert Secret on creating engaging introductions for 16 ideas to get you thinking about what you will ask people to share.

How this information is shared can be as straightforward as random shout-outs or working methodically around the table. But it can be more creative too, as with these ideas:

- Display the opener on a slide and hang chart paper for people to graffiti their responses on.
- Form mixed quads to discuss detailed replies to an intriguing question opener.
- Form trios to brainstorm and report out their response to a novelty opener.
- Display a numbered list of questions and have each person draw a playing card to determine which introduction question they will answer.

Expert Secret:
16 Ideas to Create Engaging Introductions

When you hold ongoing meetings for teams, your opening introductions beg for variety to break the monotony. Decide what the intention of your introductions will be—relax the group, build bonds, reveal perspectives, learn about one another, and so on—and then plan accordingly, These 16 ideas in four categories can inspire your thinking:

- **Intriguing questions**
  - What three words of advice would you give to a new board member?
  - What burning question do you have for the team's veteran members?
  - How would you describe your experience on this team in one sentence?
  - What one thing is holding you back in your work this week?
- **Superlatives**
  - My most useful skill is my ability to . . .
  - The best resource I have for X is . . .
  - The funniest thing I witnessed this week was . . .
  - The project responsibility I least want is . . .
- **Novelty**
  - If my portion of this project were a movie, its title would be . . .
  - If you wrote a country song about my role on this project, the lyrics would be . . .
  - This meeting's meme should read . . .
  - If I summarized this project on a bumper sticker, it would read . . .
- **Perceptions**
  - I am feeling . . .
  - I could really use . . .
  - I am excited about . . .
  - I dread . . .

Come Here Often? Initial Meetings of New Groups

When the people in your meeting don't already know one another—whether they are coming together for a single meeting or the first of many—you may be tempted to think *this* is where you will use the "standard" introductions of name and title. Although sharing these two vital pieces of information can be a start, don't let it be your end. Build on these two basics with information that will be useful to you and the meeting members. Consider these ideas:

- In the first of multiple meetings for a new project team, add "and a strength I bring to this project is . . ." to name and title.
- If the group is only meeting once, adding "and a resource I am in need of is . . ." or "and a challenge I am seeking solutions to right now is . . ." will create opportunities for participants to benefit personally from attending your meeting.
- When the participants come from different organizations, you might add "and unique resources I can tap into through my organization are . . ." to name and title.

>>> **Reality Check:** Are your introductions—when you have them—limited to names and titles?

>>> **Bottom Line:** Plan introductions, and the time they will require, by balancing such factors as the overall meeting length, the formality of the meeting, what you want to achieve with the introductions, and what the meeting members' needs are—do they need a reprieve from the gravity of their task, a jolt of lightheartedness, an opportunity to voice frustrations or share accomplishments, or something else?

To Sum Up Proactively Managing Bad Behavior

You have seen the behaviors before. You know what to expect. The difference now that you have read Chapter 3 is that you recognize how to prevent many of them. Use the chapters' 50+ techniques in three categories—seating, charts, openings—to head off meeting meltdowns and exponentially reduce the headaches you need to manage reactively. Chapter 4 will help you with those that do surface.

Put It Into Practice

Preventing Bad Behavior With Your Opener

When you developed your agenda at the end of Chapter 2, did you include a welcome as one of your agenda items? If you did, do you still believe it is the *right* opener for your meeting? Did you allocate the appropriate amount of time for it? If so, skip this page and continue on. If not, take the time now to plan your opener based on the type of meeting you are leading and the ideas in this chapter.

Meeting Type:

- ❒ Bad News Meeting
- ❒ Continuous Meeting
- ❒ New Meeting

Planned Meeting Opening/Welcome:

Note, your agenda items and overall meeting timing in your draft agenda may now require updating to accommodate the opening you just planned.

Preventing Bad Behavior

Need this chapter's essence in a minute? Here it is:

GET RESULTS

- Gather members' project-related strengths during opening introductions to align skills with responsibilities.
- Chart meeting progress on an agreements chart to maintain momentum and focus.
- Have and use facilitation tools such as multiple marker colors, playing cards, index cards, and a stop watch to stay ahead of disruptive behavior.

ENGAGE

- Set a plan for effective seating—whether it is random, partial random, targeted positioning, or selective positioning—instead of defaulting to open seating and the inherent challenges that accompany it.
- Consider adding an element of novelty to introductions for ongoing meetings to energize the group and infuse levity.
- Gather members' interests during opening introductions to involve them eagerly in ways they will enjoy.
- Chart social agreements on a displayed guidelines chart.

INSPIRE

- Watch for and develop a set of stories, quotes, and statistics that you can draw from to set a neutral climate when opening bad news meetings.
- Demonstrate your commitment to creating great meetings by paying attention to details such as coordinating seating to achieve greater effectiveness.

- Invite members to share a need they have during opening introductions—one for which others may have solutions.
- Chart off-topic items that are raised on a concerns chart and revisit them for action at the meeting's close.

"Remember, action today can prevent
a crisis tomorrow."
—*Steve Shallenberger*

Find more at www.KimberlyDevlin.com.

How Do I Manage Disruptive Meeting Behaviors?

13 Techniques to Get a Derailed Meeting Back on Track

"It is easy to sit up and take notice.
What is difficult is getting up and taking action."
—Honoré de Balzac

Ben Franklin wisely said that an ounce of prevention is worth a pound of cure. If you turned directly here to ease a pain point associated with managing misconduct in your meetings, I will ask you to take a step back to Chapter 3, which gives you proactive behavior management strategies. Your first action to manage poor behavior should always be to prevent it.

But even with preemptive action, some counterproductive behaviors can still surface. Left unchecked they can derail your meeting. So, for those times when you can't head off difficult behaviors at the pass, this chapter addresses how to manage nine consistently demonstrated behavior challenges: arriving late, disengaging, wisecracking, presenting hidden agendas, dominating, having side conversations, going on tangents, leaving early, and failing to volunteer for tasks.

Your participants are counting on you to provide a safe and productive space to engage with each other and to accomplish results. Dealing with disruptive behavior in a positive, respectful way will contribute greatly toward a successful and effective meeting.

Choose to Believe the Best: The Secret Weapon of Behavior Management

Before we tackle the nine disruptive behaviors, think about the potential sources of such conduct—other than a reliably difficult personality—and consider how a behavior's trigger can influence your reaction to it. What else could be going on besides a meeting member holding a grudge, wanting your initiative to fail, resisting participating to make a point, and other jerk moves? What does the view look like if you observe your meeting from the participants' viewpoints instead of your own? Let your answers to these questions set a positive intention in you.

Recognize that not all bad behavior stems from bad intention—when you label an action as a deliberate confrontational act, everything about your reaction to it is affected—your tone, body language, choice of words, even your endocrine system's adrenaline response. Conversely, when you approach disruptive behaviors with the belief that the behavior is unintentional (in effect, giving your participants the benefit of the doubt), it will positively influence how your intervention is delivered, received, and perceived. For more on why people are disruptive and how you can manage their disruptions, check out the Expert Secret on the next page.

Build a Better Mousetrap: Effective Strategies to Manage Disruptive Behaviors

Perhaps as common as the bad behaviors themselves are the ineffective and awkward interventions typically used to address them. Possibly out of desperation, many meeting leaders resort to thinly veiled sarcasm or awkward transitions. They use phrases such as: "Do you have something to share with everyone?," "Glad you decided to join us," and "Does anyone other than

Expert Secret:
The Root of All Evil Isn't Always Evil

Although it may feel like it in the moment, not all bad behavior stems from bad intention. Challenging behaviors can also be attributed to neutral or even positive aspects of your participants' circumstances, including being enthusiastic, unaware, high-ranking, or indifferent. Let's look at what might be behind these four triggers of disruptive behavior and how each calls for subtle—but significant—differences in your reaction. In all instances, your unwavering sincerity will be key.

Eagerness

An enthusiastic meeting member is great to have—until his excitement crosses over into excess and becomes a liability. When he gets caught up in the work, he may lose track of time, dominate the discussion, or take the group on tangents. For the overeager participant, compliment his zeal when addressing his behavior. Keep in mind that you want to temper his enthusiasm, not shut him down. Try this: "James, your passion for this is evident—and is an incredible asset to the project—for the next 10 minutes I will ask that we stay focused on the second agenda item."

Lack of Awareness

Unaware of the effect of her actions, the participant who takes a call, disconnects from group work to reply to messages, or carries on a pantomimed conversation with a person outside the glass-walled conference room often doesn't realize she is causing a disruption. Using a cause-and-effect statement when addressing her behavior will help her recognize your reason for taking action. It can be as simple as: "Debbie, we can see that you have an important issue to address. Why don't you step out and manage it—so that we can work productively—and then rejoin us when you are able to focus on this again."

High-Ranking Position

Senior managers are accustomed to doing the talking and holding peoples' attention, so don't get rattled by their interruptions. Connect with this participant informally before the meeting—even if your only opportunity is in the few minutes leading to the start time. During the meeting, use

Continued on next page

Continued from previous page

phrases such as: "Exactly, Karl, we spoke previously on this and you are correct—I'd like to get the groups' perspective too before we head there. Are you OK with that?" Or try: "Yes, you are just one step ahead of us—that is where we are going next" or "Thank you for bringing that up—I did consider that and was a bit surprised to learn. . . ." Acknowledge his position and contribution but gently guide attention to the matter at hand—your agenda.

Indifference

In this case, at best, your meeting is simply not the participant's current priority; at worst, she just doesn't care—and possibly never will. Consider if she can be excused from the meeting or removed from the group—which may do you both a favor. If she is there to stay, talk with her privately. Start by asking if extenuating circumstances are driving her behavior and respond accordingly. If they are not, clarify why she has been included and the expectations for her participation. The expert tip here is to spin these to her perspective: How will *she* gain from engaging and contributing productively? It may be as basic as maintaining or gaining respect from her peers. Either win her over or minimize her pain—and thereby yours!

Karen have something to add?" Don't worry if you have ever said something similar when faced with disruptive behavior. There are better strategies, however, that you can develop for your meeting toolkit. Start from the belief that the behavior is inadvertent instead of malicious, draw on your meeting tools from Chapters 2 and 3—agenda, concerns chart, and guidelines chart—and use the practical strategies shared here to manage the behaviors. In this way, you will engage and inspire participants—not embarrass them—as you address counterproductive conduct.

Here are the nine common disruptive behaviors we are going to tackle in this chapter: arriving late, disengaging, using too much humor, presenting hidden agendas, dominating the discussion, engaging in sidebar conversations, going on tangents, leaving early, and failing to volunteer for action items. Before we discuss each in turn, take a moment to reflect on how you currently handle these behaviors in your meetings (Tool 4-1).

Tool 4-1: Strategies Currently Used to Manage Disruptive Behaviors

Imagine a meeting so challenging that you encounter all nine disruptive behaviors listed below. Complete the worksheet with specific examples of what you usually do and say to manage each behavior.

Disruptive Behaviors	My Go-To Reaction to Manage the Behavior
Arrives late	
Disengages	
Uses too much humor	
Presents a hidden agenda	
Dominates the discussion	
Engages in a sidebar conversation	
Goes on tangents	
Leaves early	
Fails to volunteer for action items	

Arrives Late

Welcome the latecomer sincerely. Make eye contact, smile, and direct her to a seat as you continue to lead the current meeting segment. Based on the timing of her arrival, assimilate her in the least disruptive way. Consider asking her subgroup to explain their task and involve her, invite the recorder to recap his notes on the agreements reached, or have a brief sidebar with her at a natural breaking point to provide a one-on-one update.

Disengages

People may disengage for many reasons, including not hearing a question, confusion over what was asked, fearing comments will be criticized, deferring to senior positions, and lack of trust, to name a few. Repeating a request, rephrasing a question, or referring to your charted "active participation" guideline may be sufficient to overcome many of these issues. If, however, these base-level actions don't get the results you need, ask an opinion question—one for which there are no wrong answers. You can also use information gathered during introductions to draw specific people into the discussion. Try: "Gloria, when you introduced yourself, you mentioned previous experience with software implementations—please tell us what presented the greatest communication opportunities and challenges in those projects."

Uses Too Much Humor

There is a place for humor and levity in meetings—after all, this book is about running meetings that people *want* to participate in as much as it is about effective meetings. The challenge comes in when a participant crosses the line into constant wisecracking. When this occurs, address the behavior directly. Try this: "You have strong skills and extensive knowledge, Lorenzo, and it is difficult to defend your credibility when you are joking all the time." Or, as you are facilitating the meeting, try this with a smile: "I enjoy a good laugh—almost as much as I enjoy ending meetings on time—and we are at risk of running over if we don't bring closure to this item."

Presents a Hidden Agenda

Bring hidden agendas into the open respectfully. You can ask: "How does this relate to our agenda?" and respond accordingly. You can also try: "I don't see the direct connection between this agenda item and our line of discussion. Let's add this to the concerns chart—I will come back to it before we wrap up."

Dominates the Discussion

This misbehavior can take one of two forms: rambling or having the predominant voice. A rambler requires—and often appreciates—assistance phrases to help her get to her point, such as: "What I'm hearing you say is . . . , is that correct?," "Is it accurate to summarize that as . . . ?," or "How would you condense that into one or two sentences?" Overbearing voices will require redirecting statements so you can firmly pivot to others in the group. Two to try are: "We have heard your thoughts on this, let's hear another perspective," or "You know, Dan, we heard from you on this already . . . Phil, you have been waiting to comment."

Engages in a Sidebar Conversation

Please *don't* ask this participant: "Do you have something to share, Curtis?" In fact, phrases are not the recommended response to this challenge; actions are. Here are four options to try: 1) pause—allow a moment for Curtis to finish; 2) move yourself—stand close to him without looking at him and continue to lead the meeting; 3) move Curtis—use the selective seating approach detailed in Chapter 3; or 4) give him a job—any job relevant to the meeting that will reengage him in the meeting. If the behavior persists, address it directly—privately or publicly as appropriate—and refer to your charted "one conversation at a time" guideline when you do.

Goes on Tangents

Take swift action when tangents surface. The longer the tangential discussion continues, the less tangential it may become to meeting participants. When warranted, ask the scribe to add it to the concerns chart or ask the recorder to document the concern as an agenda item for the next meeting. Otherwise, redirect the group back to your meeting's Purpose (Chapter 1).

Try: "I am following you, and I also need to bring us back to the agenda." When appropriate to exercise a bit of peer pressure, try this: "To ensure we end on time, I am going to have to stop you there."

Leaves Early

As with late arrivals, be considerate and do not judge the reason for the early departure. To keep your meeting productive and ensure that the work done in this person's absence is not undone after the fact, try this: "Before you go, can we get your commitment to support the agreements we reach without your input?"

If he lets you know in advance that he will be leaving early, share the remaining agenda items, ask him to provide his ideas to another person present, and request his commitment to stand by the group's choices. As he stands to leave, publicly thank him for extending his support of the group's decisions—this formalizes his stance and communicates to the group that the work performed from here on *will* matter.

Fails to Volunteer for Action Items

When participants are unwilling to take ownership of after-meeting actions, try these three strategies that exert increasing degrees of control over the situation. Start with: "The only thing keeping us from wrapping up is getting these action items assigned." If needed, continue with the Do The Math technique: Compare the number of items to the number of people and do the math. For example: "There are six action items and 12 of us. If we do the math, that means we can work in pairs so all six items are completed." And, finally, the least preferred recourse is making direct work assignments. If you must resort to this option, make every effort to connect action items to the strengths shared by each person during meeting introductions.

>>> **Reality Check:** There will always be naysayers, interrupters, monopolizers, and others who get in the way of progress during meetings.

>>> **Bottom Line:** Don't take it personally. Stay the course. You might even consider adding this Chinese proverb to your guidelines chart: "Those who say it cannot be done should not interrupt those doing it."

To Sum Up Managing Disruptive Behaviors

Another proverb, this one from Japan, says it well: "Fall seven times and stand up eight." Managing meeting behaviors requires tenacity to be able to react firmly, intentionally, and consistently. It also requires decorum and respect—for the offender, the other meeting participants, and yourself. Without decorum and respect, your intervening behaviors can themselves become distractions.

Expert Secret:
Your Go Bag of Ready Responses

In the moment, it can be difficult to think of the right words to say to respond to disruptions eloquently and respectfully. Just as you have a "go bag" for emergency situations, prepare a personalized go bag of phrases to have ready when needed. Practice them until they become second nature. Here are a few to get you started:

- ☐ "I am sorry you were running late and am glad that you are here now. We have a seat for your right here."
- ☐ "How does this line of discussion support our meeting outcomes?"
- ☐ "I'd like to wrap this up and move forward."
- ☐ "We have heard from you on this issue and would like to open up the floor to others."

A quick-reference cheat sheet for managing meeting meltdowns is included in the *Meeting Expert's Toolkit Bundle* available for purchase at www.KimberlyDevlin.com.

Put It Into Practice

Redefined Strategies to Manage Disruptive Behaviors

The Roman playwright Plautus said: "Things we do not expect, happen more frequently than we wish." Expect bad behavior—and have a plan for when it presents itself. Your personalized behavior-management plan will be critical to conducting meetings that inspire, engage, and get results—without first being reduced to schoolyard scuffles or street fights. Consider an upcoming meeting and who will be participating. What disruptive actions can you anticipate? How will you react? What will you *say*? What will you *do*? Complete the worksheet with specific examples—refer to the previous pages for suggestions as well as the strategies you noted in Tool 4-1.

Disruptive Behaviors	My New Plan to Manage the Behavior
Arrives late	
Disengages	
Uses too much humor	
Presents a hidden agenda	
Dominates the discussion	
Engages in a sidebar conversation	
Goes on tangents	
Leaves early	
Fails to volunteer for action items	

Managing Disruptive Behaviors

Need this chapter's essence in a minute? Here it is:

GET RESULTS

- Gather members' project-related strengths during opening introductions to enable you to align their talents with task assignments when volunteers may be scarce.
- Find a healthy balance point between taskmaster and merrymaker as the meeting's leader.
- Respond to disruptive situations respectfully and with a collaborative—not confrontational—attitude.
- Address disruptive behaviors quickly—before they escalate and become more challenging to manage.
- Recognize that tenacity may be required.

ENGAGE

- Address the behavior without attacking the person.
- Let your first assumption be that participants are well intended and want to contribute productively.
- Demonstrate deference for participants in senior positions to maintain their buy-in, support, and participation.
- Use body language—eye contact, facial expressions, movement—to supplement, or in place of, what you say when presented with challenging behaviors.

INSPIRE

- Demonstrate respect for all meeting participants at all times.
- Recognize not all bad behavior stems from bad intention—when you label an action as a deliberate confrontational

act, everything about your reaction to it is affected—your tone, body language, choice of words, even your endocrine system's adrenaline response.

- Set a positive intention as you address disruptive behaviors—it will influence how you manage the behaviors, how others receive your reactions, and how you are perceived by the group.

"Every action has an impact;
choose wisely the impact you want to have."
—*Mindy Hall*

Find more at www.KimberlyDevlin.com.

We Had the Meeting—
Now What?

The Three-Step Method to
Ensure Follow-Through

"In golf, as in life, it's the follow-through
that makes the difference."
—Ben Wicks

Whew! Your meeting is over. You planned it, you led it, you managed it, you survived it—time to celebrate? Not quite. All your efforts leading up to the meeting and your finesse facilitating the meeting will be of little value without follow-through and follow-up (two different things, by the way). Here is the great news: There is very little you need to do now to initiate post-meeting action and confirm that action has been taken. All your efforts related to earlier chapters' strategies and techniques have set you up for success here. Want some more good news? Because most of your work is already done, this chapter is a quick and easy read!

Ensuring Follow-Through in Three Easy Steps

The three-step method to ensure follow-through is surprisingly simple: 1) gain agreement from each person on next steps; 2) finalize and distribute a summary of discussion; and 3) confirm completion of actions. You can do this—with a little help from this chapter.

Step One: Gain Verbal Agreement

The first mistake meeting leaders make when it comes to follow-through is assuming that each person who actively participated in the meeting will leave with the same understanding of what is going to happen next. Such an assumption is logical enough—you all heard the same things, bantered ideas together, came to agreements, charted agreements, and distributed tasks with deadlines among those present—but such an assumption is also inaccurate.

Step One is to obtain a verbal report out from each person. Every meeting member in turn either states what they are going to do, when they will do it, and how they will update the team, or states their commitment to follow through with a behavior change being asked of everyone present (for example, follow a new procedure, apply new standards to every transaction, or complete an online training program by the end of the month).

In the first instance, you might try: "To close, we have one final and critical action to complete. We have been very productive today, and to avoid disconnects after we leave, I'd like each of us in turn to share what we have committed to do, our deadlines for completing them, as well as our degree of certainty we will meet those deadlines. I will go first. . . ."

In the second situation, try: "Thank you all for your collaboration and sharing your concerns to get your questions answered. Now that we have worked through what your revised responsibilities look like—[*summarize them as actions*]—I want to ensure we are all on the same page. I'd like each of you either to tell me you are able to and will implement these changes starting today, or to share with me what obstacle will prevent you from meeting the revised expectations. Christine, will you get us started?"

This in-meeting action—part of next steps (see Chapter 2)—looks a lot like what happens pre-flight at an airplane's exit row—the flight attendant asks each passenger for a verbal acknowledgment that they are able and willing to help in the event of an emergency—nodding isn't sufficient. It won't be sufficient in your meetings either.

If asking each person to make a verbal commitment to follow through is new to you, once completed you may feel well positioned for success. Let me ask you this though: Have you followed through on absolutely everything you said you were going to do this month, this week, today? If your answer is no, chances are that some things—even those you wanted and intended to do—simply slipped your mind. If your answer was yes, I'm considering hiring a personal assistant—want the job? The verbal commitment is significant—it is also not enough. And that takes us to the next step.

Step Two: Finalize the Summary of Discussion

The documentation that follows a meeting is just as important as your preparation work before the meeting. Step Two—the summary of discussion—measures the success of the meeting, defines next steps, and drives the direction of the next meeting, if there will be one. It does this by connecting the notes and decisions from the meeting to the outcomes you created. If outcomes were not achieved, it will be evident in the summary. This form of meeting documentation holds meeting leaders accountable for results and meeting members accountable for action items.

Review the Summary of Discussion Template (Tool 5-1) and see just how familiar the tool's elements are. You already generated much of the information it includes in your agenda—meeting title, day, date, time, location, members and their functions, and meeting outcomes. During the meeting, the recorder will add relevant information in the tool's space dedicated to outcomes, action items, and the next meeting.

Ideally, the summary of discussion will be distributed within 24 hours of the meeting. Here is how you can achieve that with little effort: Pre-fill the template with data from your agenda and provide an e-version to the meeting's recorder. During the meeting, ask the recorder to type relevant information and decisions under each outcome, capture action items in the designated space, and make note of the agreed date and time of the next meeting—directly in the file. After the meeting, review the draft, edit it for clarity and accuracy as required, and distribute it to the meeting members via email. The savvy meeting leader will do one more thing. Instead of hitting "send" and checking off this task, to inspire, engage, and get results, close your email with a confirmation request. Try this: "Please confirm that you have reviewed the attached and that it accurately represents the meeting. If anything is missing or incorrect, please notify me."

Tool 5-1: Summary of Discussion Template

Meeting Title	
Day/Date/Time	
Location	
Meeting Members/ Function	
Meeting Outcomes	1. 2. 3.
Outcome #1	*Copy Outcome #1 here, from above*
Outcome #2	*Copy Outcome #2 here, from above*
Outcome #3	*Copy Outcome #3 here, from above*
Next Steps	Action Items: • • • Next Meeting: •

Step Three: Follow Up on Follow-Through

The meeting participants said they would do "it," you sent a summary of discussion that recorded it, they confirmed receipt and their agreement with it—surely you must now be finished? Not so fast. At the beginning of the chapter, I mentioned that *follow-through* and *follow-up* are two different things. The former is the action itself; the latter is confirming the action happened or is happening as planned—and it is Step Three.

To streamline follow-up, set an expectation that meeting members will circle back and confirm they have completed their action items. Do this during the meeting and in your summary of discussion's transmission email. Tracking action items may be performed through a team collaboration app or software, or it can be centrally managed—with each member notifying a designated person of their progress. You will want to connect with anyone who has open items or has not reported their progress.

For meetings held with staff to set new performance expectations or such, it will be your responsibility to confirm team members are acting in accordance with the new guidelines as well as to support them during their transition to a new normal. Behavior change doesn't happen overnight in a vacuum—the standard may be set that quickly, but performance support will be required as employees get used to the change.

〉〉〉 **Reality Check:** Do the decisions made and agreements reached during meetings seem impossible to forget or confuse at a later date? Do you breathe a sigh of relief at the end of your meetings and head off to your next appointment confident that the team who just committed to taking action is heading off to do exactly that?

〉〉〉 **Bottom Line:** Memories fade, recollections get skewed, and many more decisions and agreements will be made after today's meeting. The summary of discussion memorializes the meeting's outcomes, serves as a reference and memory jogger, and provides a tangible to-do list for each person in the meeting. It is a critical tool for all meetings.

To Sum Up the Three-Step Method to Ensure Follow-Through

After the initial work you completed to plan your meeting, the potential challenges you addressed during it, and the time you dedicated to the meeting, it would be a shame to lose your focus on getting results now. Develop a three-step habit of asking meeting members to make a verbal announcement of their next steps; distributing a summary of discussion with decisions and action items that everyone who was in attendance understands, agrees to, and has a role in supporting; and confirming that those actions happened.

ONE-MINUTE ROUNDUP

Ensuring Follow-Through

Need this chapter's essence in a minute? Here it is:

GET RESULTS

- Follow-through and follow-up are two different things: follow-through is the action itself; follow-up is confirming the action happened as planned. For real results, remain focused on both.
- Provide the recorder with the pre-filled summary of discussion template to streamline his work during the meeting, create a consistent format, and ease your work finalizing the summary after the meeting.
- Distribute the summary of discussion within 24 hours of the meeting.

ENGAGE

- Do not assume that each person who actively participated in the same meeting you were in will leave with the same understanding of what is going to happen next.
- When action items have been assigned, ask participants to share what they have committed to do, their deadlines for completing them, and their degree of certainty that they will meet the deadlines.
- When new performance expectations have been set, ask each person to individually confirm they are able to and intend to comply with the new requirements—or describe any obstacles that will prevent them from doing so.

INSPIRE

- Here, I want you to be inspired that your efforts up until now will pay off at this critical stage. PLANNER, your well-crafted agenda, and your skillful management of meeting behaviors before and during the meeting set you up for success with ensuring follow-through—when you have done the preparatory work, the hardest part of ensuring follow-through is over.
- Set the example when you ask meeting members to share a verbal commitment at the meeting's close—be the first to report out and be sure to complete your action items.
- Close summary of discussion transmission emails with this request: "Please confirm that you have reviewed the attached and that it accurately represents the meeting. If anything is missing or incorrect, please notify me."

"Many people don't focus enough on execution.
If you make a commitment to get something done,
you need to follow through on that commitment."
— Kenneth I. Chenault

Find more at www.KimberlyDevlin.com.

What About Meetings Disguised as Conversations?

Applying *Don't Waste My Time* Tools to Your One-on-One Meetings

"The preparation is what allows the success to happen naturally."
—Jake Arrieta

In the interest of full disclosure, this chapter assumes you have worked through previous chapters' ideas and strategies and are now ready to tailor them to your one-on-one meetings—aka conversations. Its guidance applies to nondisciplinary meetings between two people. Impromptu conversations and progressive discipline discussions each have recommended best practices of their own and are not the focus here.

During meetings of two people, one person commonly leads the conversation. Chapter 6 is directed to that person—who will not always be the more senior person. When you hold the authority to convene a one-on-one meeting—with an employee, a vendor, and so on—it is likely you will also lead the conversation. When you have requested the one-on-one meeting—of your boss, a prospect, or a peer—leading it may well be your responsibility, regardless of your respective titles.

Much remains consistent from your larger meetings to those of only two people. For both, you need to prepare with the PLANNER framework, plan the conversation's agenda, stay ahead of disruptive behavior, address challenges that may arise, and follow through after the discussion. What is different is how some of these actions are achieved. Read on to learn how to plan and lead one-on-one meetings that inspire, engage, and get results.

PLANNER Applied to One-on-One Meetings

All successful meetings, no matter the size, are the result of planning based on Purpose, Location, Agenda, Names, Note-taking, Expectations, and Responsibilities—the PLANNER framework. It is a mistake to consider one-on-one meetings less formal and therefore be less structured in your preparation for them. Although your *demeanor* may be more informal and the meeting may *feel* more informal, your planning for it should not be. Here is a quick rundown of what meeting size does and does not change or influence in PLANNER.

Purpose

Risking redundancy, I will quote Steve Jobs again: "You should never go to a meeting or make a telephone call without a clear idea of what you are trying to achieve." Never. Without this knowledge you are wasting your time and someone else's. Writing specific tangible or observable outcomes defines what you are trying to achieve. Yes, *writing* them—do actually write them before the conversation. And then share them early in the conversation.

Knowing that many one-on-one meetings have a purpose related to gathering expertise or specialized knowledge, receiving an approval, or reaching agreement on a future course of action may help you to answer purpose's key question: "What do I need to achieve with this meeting?"

Location

With only two people participating, a phone call becomes a tempting alternative to your physical options: "my" work space, "your" work space, or a neutral space. A phone call can be convenient, but it doesn't have the benefit of using body language and the other person may be multi-tasking instead of giving you his full attention. Meeting in person shows a sign of respect, brings body language into the conversation, and allows you to redirect the conversation based on visual cues. The greatest drawback to meeting face-to-face is that travel may be required. Choose your location based on how well it supports achieving your outcomes instead of convenience.

Agenda

Even one-on-one meetings benefit from an agenda. Remember, your agenda is your path through the meeting—the processes to achieve your desired outcomes—which may or may not be distributed in one-on-one meetings (more on this later in the chapter).

Names

The three key actions associated with names in Chapter 1 are to determine the participants' contribution to achieving the outcomes, whether they will have decision-making authority, and if a representative can be sent in their place. How hard could this be for a one-on-one meeting? There are only two of you—or will there be? It is a best practice to confirm whether any other people will be participating. A simple "Will anyone be joining us?" sets you up to effectively plan for the meeting. Completing the three key Names actions from Chapter 1—even for one-on-one meetings—will ensure you are preparing to speak with the *right* person.

Note-taking

Regardless of meeting size, notes need to be taken. A results-driven meeting has a complete written account of its decisions and agreed-upon next steps that all in attendance acknowledge accurately represents the meeting—even if there are just two of you.

What *does* change potentially regarding note-taking is who does it. Let hierarchy drive this. When meeting with a peer or person senior to you, record the discussion yourself. When you manage or supervise the other person in the meeting, it may be appropriate to delegate the responsibility to her—especially if the meeting addresses a new work assignment or a performance issue. Another change for one-on-one meetings is that the separate scribe function—that is, charting the work of the participants—won't apply.

Expectations

What *doesn't* change? The expectations. You will still be expected to be prepared, start and end on time, be engaging (think two-way dialogue versus one-way monologue), stay focused, set meeting boundaries, and remain open to alternative views. It is also fair for you to expect the other person to be prepared, engage in the discussion, remain constructive, achieve clarity on next steps, and follow through. The need to *communicate* expectations also doesn't change; to hold people accountable, the expectations must first be set.

What *does* change? *How* the expectations are communicated. The best communication strategy for your meeting will depend on the meeting's purpose, the relationship between the two parties, the history leading up to the conversation, whether you requested or convened the meeting, and so on. Think through how your meeting's circumstances should drive your choices. Some expectations may be shared at the outset and others at natural points during the meeting. Beginning by telling a client or prospect that you expect his full participation isn't advisable, but saying that you'd like to hear his thoughts will set the same expectation respectfully.

Responsibilities

In meetings of many people, the leader who attempts to perform all the meeting's responsibilities becomes its Sherpa, carrying the load for everyone, which is exhausting and not advisable. In a meeting of two people, though, the leader is accountable for everything—with the possible exception of note-taking, discussed previously. In this setting, you are responsible for leading, managing time, troubleshooting, ensuring both people contribute, and any additional roles that are required to support your outcome. The two super-fluous roles in one-on-one meetings are those of facilitator and scribe. If a facilitator is needed—and she might be (think mediator)—you are no longer planning a one-on-one meeting.

>>> **Reality Check:** Do you look at one-on-one meetings as informal and therefore not requiring preparation? Do you believe that you will get similar or better results with an impromptu approach?

>>> **Bottom Line:** Meetings that inspire, engage, and get results are characterized by meeting leaders who put thought, time, and effort into designing an effective event—even if only two people are involved. The time you invest *before* your meeting to work through the PLANNER framework will pay off exponentially during and after your one-on-one meetings.

> "It usually takes me more than three weeks to prepare
> a good impromptu speech."
> —Mark Twain

Agendas for One-On-One Meetings

The value of a well-crafted agenda is that it establishes your objectives, drives the meeting's processes, and keeps the meeting on track—all things you want for your one-on-one meetings. Whether you use the agenda template available in the *Meeting Expert's Toolkit Bundle* at www.KimberlyDevlin.com or your own, building an agenda is mission critical for all meetings. If the meeting is important enough to have, it deserves an agenda.

What may differ in your one-on-one meetings is whether the agenda is *distributed*. I recently led two one-on-one meetings of four hours. The first was exploratory and held to obtain specialized knowledge from a subject matter resource. The second was a train-the-trainer held to reach agreement on future action (how the course will be led). I shared a printed agenda in the second meeting but not the first. For both meetings, I created and printed my leader's agendas. They included my outcomes, an outline of the flow we'd follow to achieve them, talking points aligned with each agenda item, and relevant details I might otherwise overlook. During both meetings, my agendas served as quick references to my goals and plans to accomplish them.

Here are a few special considerations for one-on-one meeting agendas related to agenda items and next steps.

You read in Chapter 2 that agenda items define your *strategy* for accomplishing your outcomes. Obviously, in a meeting of only two people, small group work, report outs, voting, and such will not be applicable processes. However, you still want your one-on-one meetings to be engaging, and there are processes to support that. Although discussion may dominate your agenda items, how can presentation, brainstorming, prioritization, data review, or demonstration move you both toward your outcomes?

Next steps take on added importance in meetings disguised as conversations. The purpose of one-on-one meetings isn't to "have a talk"—it is to achieve your outcomes. Without follow-through and follow-up, real results after the talk are unlikely. The next steps portion of your conversation solidifies the agreements reached and then sets a plan for actions discussed. Potential disconnects commonly reveal themselves at this point and may sound like: "Oh, I assumed you'd be handling that," "I guess I heard you wrong," or "OK, I thought we said by the 15th not the 5th." Listen for these opportunities to clarify, revisit agreements to ensure consensus, and confirm both parties share the same post-meeting expectations.

>>> **Reality Check:** Does time spent planning your one-on-one meeting seem like wasted time or overkill?

>>> **Bottom Line:** Having an agenda demonstrates your preparedness, frees you to focus on the discussion during the meeting, and gets you results more quickly.

Preventing Bad Behavior in One-on-One Meetings

When you think about dealing with bad behavior, you probably envision *other* people's actions in meetings. Checking your own conduct and emotions will be essential in one-on-one meetings, where you are exactly one-half of the equation. Don't be the one to create obstacles through tone, expressions, gestures, or other body language. You will also want to leverage the tools introduced in Chapter 3: seating, charts, and openings.

Seating

Nothing about seating arrangements in Chapter 3 applies to your one-on-one meetings! Meetings of two people require their own seating considerations and, unless you are on a phone call, navigating furniture will be involved. Let's consider three such environments: an office, a conference room, or another neutral space—cafeteria, break room, coffee shop, or such. You will want to consider your desired outcomes and agenda items as well as the insights that follow to make your best seating choice.

In an office, sitting across from one another with a desk between you is considered combative. It establishes one person as "in charge," and it can generate defensiveness and confrontational thinking and behavior. Sitting beside one another, on the same side of the desk, creates a collaborative atmosphere and is perceived as a cooperative position to work through challenges, work together on a task, review data together, and so on.

Conference room tables provide an office's two options—and the same guidelines apply. They also offer two additional arrangements: the corner position and sitting diagonal to one another. The corner position—elbow-to-elbow with each of you on perpendicular sides of the table—is seen as friendly. It supports eye contact and collaboration and has the added benefit of allowing for both casual and more formal agenda items, such as presentations. When a person sits diagonally across a conference table though, the message his body language conveys is commonly interpreted as disinterest, indifference, or hostility. Avoid taking this position and change the configuration before starting your meeting if the other person chooses such a seat—either by repositioning yourself or with something like: "Sitting over here will actually be more conducive to the agenda I have planned, if you don't mind."

Tables in other neutral spaces vary. Their shape—square, rectangular, round—and size will dictate your options. For round tables, the corner position doesn't exist, but the confrontational seat does—it remains directly across the table. At a round table, the disinterested position is any seat far away while not being directly across, and the collaborative position is side by side.

Furniture's relative position to the room adds other dynamics in these neutral spaces. Will you choose a table central to activity or off to the side? Whose back may face a door? Who will or won't have a view of people coming and going from the space? And what affect might these choices have on your agenda items? Meeting spaces selected for neutrality can become impediments to achieving your outcomes if not chosen thoughtfully.

Even with phone call meetings, seating can be a factor. Will you sit or stand? If you sit, will you maintain a forward posture or recline and relax into your chair? Will you sit at your desk or in another chair to potentially open yourself up to other perspectives? Your choices will influence your tone, energy, and more—all of which can be heard through the phone line.

Charts

In one-on-one meetings, strategic use of a notepad can take the place of wall charts for guidelines, agreements, and concerns. Although charting social agreements would be awkward, they should be established. Consider both personalities and your meeting goals, and then choose the few guidelines that will be most critical, such as: stay focused, remain open-minded, limit the discussion to things within our control, or others. As you share them, write them on your pad under an underlined heading: Guidelines. When the two of you come to your first agreement, mark a section of your pad "Agreements," underline the heading, and write the decision as you explain what you are doing. Similarly, if an unrelated issue comes up, flip to a fresh sheet and record the item beneath your third underlined heading: "Concerns." The act of recording these meeting elements is equally critical in one-on-one meetings to elevate their importance and to serve as touchpoints to return to should challenges need to be managed.

Openings

Most interactions between two people begin with social niceties, and your one-on-one meetings will be no different. What can be tricky, at times, is transitioning to the purpose of the meeting. Chapter 3 introduced four categories for creating engaging introductions—intriguing questions, superlatives, novelty, and perceptions—that you can modify to move seamlessly from chitchat to the purpose of the conversation. When meeting with an employee to discuss a performance issue related to her judgement, for example, you might transition with this altered intriguing question: "What would you say are the top priorities that should drive the decisions you make in your position?" When meeting with a peer to work on a special assignment, you might transition with this superlative question: "Which of your skills do you think will be most useful on this project?" To move a client into the meeting, you could ask a novelty question such as this: "What is your word of the day related to [*your product or service*]?" And, lastly, to integrate perceptions into any one-on-one meeting's opening, try: "I'd really like to hear your thoughts on X," or "I need a fresh perspective on this, can you help me see X differently?"

I recommend knowing verbatim what you will say or ask to transition into the meeting. Preferably it will be something that requires a response to begin the two-way discussion.

>>> **Reality Check:** Think problems can't surface in meetings of two people?

>>> **Bottom Line:** Think again. And plan accordingly using these strategies tailored to one-on-one meetings.

Managing Disruptive Behavior in One-on-One Meetings

It would be convenient if one-on-one meetings were somehow exempt from disruptions caused by their two participants. In reality, they aren't. Whether characterized as a pleasant conversation with a person whose company you enjoy or a tense—even contentious—conversation, one-on-one meetings can require you to manage disruptions. The challenges that plague larger meetings can be equally disruptive to conversations—they just may take on distinctive appearances in the smaller setting. Tangents can sound like stream-of-conscious chatter—but they still take you off task. Disengaging can look like multi-tasking, allowing interruptions, or being more attentive to what is happening nearby than the conversation itself—but it still disrupts the flow of the discussion. And, too much humor can feel like catching up with a friend—but it still restricts productivity.

Loss of focus attributed to these and other challenges in one-on-one meetings may go unnoticed more easily without the crowd of a larger meeting expressing frustration. So, stay alert. Recognize and react to behavior shifts as they are occurring, and place greater emphasis on what body language communicates than the words being said when the two are incongruent. With your one-on-one meetings, taking a break or planning to reconvene at another time become viable options—in fact, I commonly begin phone meetings with the question: "Is this still a good time for you?" If it isn't, I don't want to begin only to find the other person distracted, rushed, or uninterested.

>>> **Reality Check**: Do you approach one-on-one meetings expecting an easy and on-time flow from one agenda item to the next?

>>> **Bottom Line**: Keeping a conversation on track can be unruly business. When you get along well, unrelated topics may be more fun and interesting than the agenda. When you don't get along, either of you may try to sidestep issues, deflect blame, avoid taking responsibility for action items, withdraw, and more. Call upon your interpersonal communication skills instead of strategies for addressing group dynamics to manage disruptions in conversations.

Three Steps to Ensure Follow-Through for One-on-One Meetings

Your execution of follow-through for a one-on-one meeting may be more informal, but its existence remains essential. The three-step method from Chapter 5 will get the job done for you with a few variations in implementation.

- **Step One: Verbal Agreement**. Transition to closing one-on-one meetings with a review of the agreements, action items, and next steps. Try: "Before we wrap up, let's review where we are. I have noted [*share agreements*], and I recorded these action items: [*list them, beginning with your own*]. In terms of next steps, we agreed that [*specify*]. Have I missed anything?"
- **Step Two: Finalize the Summary of Discussion.** Yes, your one-on-one meetings need a summary of discussion too. And it should still be sent within 24 hours of the conversation. But, it may be appropriate to use a more informal structure, as demonstrated in the sidebar example from a call with my publisher that follows. Notice that all of the key elements are included, and the attendees and location are inferred in the opening.

- **Step Three: Follow Up on Follow-Through.** Reach agreement at the end of a one-on-one meeting on how you will follow up with each other on your action items. Frequently, I use the emailed summary of discussion as a tracking tool, noting "done" beside items as completed. For ongoing collaborations, you can open meetings with a review of the action items from the previous meeting's summary of discussion.

>> **Reality Check:** Wondering when you will write a summary of discussion for each one-on-one meeting?

>> **Bottom Line:** Work efficiently by building an outline of your summary as you create your agenda. During the discussion, record notes and actions under the appropriate headings, and then take a few minutes after your call or meeting to proofread, finalize, and send the document. A summary of discussion is a critical tool for all meetings—even those disguised as conversations.

To Sum Up One-on-One Meetings

Although often less formal, one-on-one meetings deserve—and require—the same planning efforts as larger meetings. Craft your agenda following the same guidelines in both instances, and factor all of the PLANNER elements into your preparation. Be mindful that your own actions will influence potential challenges and disruptions because you now make up half of the participant list, and differences in personalities and communication styles can become more noticeable. Finally, set yourself apart as a meeting leader who gets results by sending a summary of discussion—what better way is there to inspire and engage people in your future one-on-one meetings than by getting results from today's?

Sample Summary of Discussion
for a One-on-One Meeting

Cat –

What a great and incredibly productive call today. Well worth the investment of two hours! We accomplished what we set out to, and more
(maybe we should be launching a book on effective meetings . . . ?).
Below is our Summary of Discussion. Please review it, confirm it matches
your notes, and acknowledge that either we are on the same page or
update as needed.

KD

~~~~~~

Meeting Title: Marketing Support and "Meetings Book" Title

Date/Time: Friday–July 20, 20xx; 1:15 to 3:15 p.m.

Meeting Outcomes:

1. Marketing plan with MR, to include:
   - List of services desired
   - Determination of how to proceed and develop work plan
     timeline
2. Agreement on three meeting book titles to poll

Outcome #1 Marketing Plan:

- Current marketing budget is $X
- Initial marketing milestone is Oct 1, 20xx
- Short-term leads goal: list of X quality contacts by October 1, 20xx
- STHT short-term sales goal: X copies via Amazon by October 31,
  20xx
- MR incentive: X% of sales on X+ units sold for six months
- **Desired services** from MR, in support of STHT, SIAH/DWMT, and
  KD.com are:
  – Marketing timeline for 30, 60, and 90 days
  – Lead generation and funnel strategy
  – Speaker marketing strategy

- Social media strategy
- Website feedback and enhancement strategies
- SEO keyword development
- **Desired deliverables** from MR, are:
    - Agreement with TPH on services/budget/schedule [next week]
    - Work plan (actions to be taken and by whom) [by Aug 1]
    - Timeline of work plan (with Oct 1, 20xx as first milestone) [by Aug 1]

Outcome #2 Meetings Book Title:

- We have a title! (and will skip polling)
- *Don't Waste My Time: Expert Secrets for Meetings That Inspire, Engage, and Get Results*

Action Items by Aug 1:

1. KD—look at video footage clips to use
2. KD—offer direction/feedback to designer on SIAH/DWMT cover
3. KD—contact AB (Ai instructor and EdTrek logo designer) about Ai student contest
4. KD—send SIAH/DWMT's draft manuscript to JB for review/input/direction (DONE)
5. CR—define incentive plan for MR
6. CR—loop back to MR to obtain agreement, work plan, and timeline based on list above
7. CR—ask MR to move forward with TED Talk opportunities
8. CR—complete contract execution with CA Link on STHT translation

Next Steps:

1. KD, JB, CR (and MR?) to define core messages/topics
2. Leverage Chinese translation of STHT once contract is complete
3. Promote upcoming SIAH/DWMT once cover art is finalized

ONE-MINUTE
ROUNDUP

One-on-One Meetings

Need this chapter's essence in a minute? Here it is:

GET RESULTS

- Recognize that for meetings of two people you still need to prepare with the PLANNER framework, plan the conversation's agenda, stay ahead of disruptive behaviors, address challenges that may arise, and follow through after the discussion.
- Your outcomes likely align with one of three purposes: gathering expertise or specialized knowledge, receiving an approval, or reaching agreement on a future course of action. Write down your outcomes for the meeting and share them early in the conversation.
- Prepare an agenda—even if you don't distribute it.
- Send a summary of discussion after the meeting and ask for confirmation that it accurately represents the discussion.

ENGAGE

- Choose a location—over the phone, "my" work space, "your" work space, or a neutral space—based on the level and type of interaction needed to achieve your outcomes.
- Consider if sharing the agenda will enhance participation or work against you based on meeting dynamics.
- Determine where you will sit—relative to one another and within the space—to most effectively achieve your outcomes.
- Plan your opening transition into the business of the meeting—one sentence, verbatim.

- Pay attention to what is being said as well as how it is said (even if you are on the phone). When the two are out of sync, prioritize the speaker's tone, pace, inflection, and volume.

INSPIRE

- Set expectations that will move you closer to achieving your outcomes.
- Rise to the other person's expectations and communicate your expectations in advance so she can be fully prepared.
- Demonstrate the importance of the meeting by making written notes of what you would otherwise chart in a larger meeting.

> *"The secret of success is to do the common thing*
> *uncommonly well."*
> *—John D. Rockefeller Jr.*

Find more at www.KimberlyDevlin.com.

Where Do I Go From Here?

Plan and Lead Meetings That Inspire, Engage, and Get Results

*"It does not matter how slowly you go
as long as you do not stop."*
—*Confucius*

M eetings that inspire, engage, and get results are within your reach! You have dedicated the time to get this far. Now, dedicate time *before* your upcoming meetings to plan for the winning events you aspire to—instead of using time *after* your meetings to wonder what went wrong.

As you have read, the secrets to successful, effective meetings are not complicated. And now that you know what they are, you can exert their powerful influence. If you consistently follow the strategies and ideas in this book, you will find not only that productivity improves but enjoyment— a word not commonly associated with meetings—increases for everyone involved:

- You can inspire meeting members instead of boring them.
- You can engage participants instead of speaking to "attendees."
- You can achieve real results instead of closing meetings with: "We can finish this up next time."

- And—the best of all—you don't have to do it on your own. I promised you support in using this book's guidance, and you can find it at www.KimberlyDevlin.com. There you will find free bonus content that supplements what you have read, a blog with articles related to this topic as well as others, and products to save you valuable time. To access practical, hands-on, small group training for meetings that *Don't Waste My Time*, connect with us at www.EdTrek.com.

Here is your Call to Action: For the next meeting you lead, do just three things to prepare: 1) complete the PLANNER worksheet; 2) build and distribute your agenda—why not pre-fill the summary of discussion template with content from the agenda while you are at it; and 3) at the same time that you block the meeting in your calendar, create a task to send the summary of discussion within 24 hours.

Then, for just-in-time reminders on preventing and managing disruptive behaviors, quickly review Chapters 3 and 4 before heading to your meeting. That's it.

Repeat the three steps for each of your meetings—they will get easier with practice. Review the strategies in Chapters 3 and 4 periodically—they will become second nature to you with repeated exposure and use. When you consistently apply the strategies of this book, you will find that far from wasting time, your meetings will inspire, engage, and get results!

> "It always seems impossible until it is done."
> —Nelson Mandela, Pliny the Elder, and others

Best of luck to you. My motivation to write books, like my drive to facilitate learning, comes from my passion to share what I have learned along the way to make the journey more fun and less challenging for those who follow. Having trained meeting leaders on the strategies in Don't Waste My Time *for more than a decade, I can tell you with confidence that the tools and techniques work—if you use them. I would enjoy reading your thoughts and comments about the ideas presented in this book—please leave a review at www.amazon.com.*

About the Author

Kimberly Devlin is an unwavering pragmatist who believes that theory alone is insufficient and time must have an ROI. She became an entrepreneur at 27 and—out of necessity—discovered ways to transform information overload and the time crunch we all face into effective, actionable behaviors that improve productivity, effectiveness, and results. With these insights, she helps clients realize business objectives through training initiatives, technical writing, strategic planning, and internal resource development. As a popular writer, instructional designer, facilitator, speaker, and consultant with more than 20 years of experience, she provides technical assistance nationally, speaks and presents at international and industry-specific conferences, and has been featured in ATD's *TD* magazine for her status as a CPLP pilot pioneer.

She is author of *Same Training, Half the Time: Delivering Results for Busy Learners* (TPH 2018) and two titles in the bestselling ATD Workshop Series: *Facilitation Skills Training* (ATD 2017) and *Customer Service Training* (ATD 2015). In addition, Kimberly writes regularly about talent development and other topics on her blog at www.KimberlyDevlin.com.

When not striking her keyboard, engaging with clients, or on a plane, she can be found reading, taking photos, or performing some active pursuit—hiking, biking, rock climbing, standup paddleboarding, dancing, or something new she hasn't tried before.

Kimberly holds an MA in journalism and a BA in English literature from the University of Miami and her Certified Professional in Learning and

Performance (CPLP) credential. She is a managing director of EdTrek, Inc., a training and development consulting firm, and president of Poetic License, Inc., a business communication consulting firm. She is a lifelong learner and receives regular reminders from her dog that there is more to life than professional accomplishments alone.

Acknowledgments

May I start by thanking you, my reader—your time is precious, the number of books you can read is limited, and yet here you are. I appreciate you making this book a priority as a path to attaining your goals. It was with readers like you in mind that we conceived the Smarter in an Hour series.

This book and series would not exist were it not for the willingness of the TPH team to indulge my request and come together on a bright November day, work collaboratively for hours, share concepts, grab markers, fill the walls with charts of stuff, and build on ideas—we were a creative powerhouse that day, and look what has come from it! Cat Russo, Jacki Edlund-Braun, Dawn Baron, and Nancy Silva—your talents and enthusiasm for what you do make working together incredibly rewarding. Our collective virtual sessions and our one-on-one phone meetings each moved *Don't Waste My Time* from concept to reality. Kristin Goble, your eye for typography and attention to detail have created inviting, easy-to-read pages. And, Patty Sloniger, what's a book without its cover? Your sharp, eye-catching design draws attention and interest.

Michelle Rabel, you have been a gift to us all. Guiding, directing, and educating, not to mention developing our skills with so many technologies. It is not the tools you brought to us but what you *did* within them and your collaborative approach that has done so much for us in so many ways. Without you, things would look different today.

And, of course, Ronnie Glotzbach—my business partner, my friend— little did we know in 2005 that *Don't Waste My Time* would be here! If a single day most significantly influenced my career's trajectory, it would be in February 2002, when Susan introduced us in LOD's conference room. A lot has happened since then. From creating EdTrek, its Journeys in Learning, and designing *The Supervisor's Apprenticeship*® together to growing the course offerings year after year and partnering with thousands of professionals seeking tools to achieve better results—*Don't Waste My Time*, the book, wouldn't exist without *Don't Waste My Time*™, the class. Just as true, Kimberly Devlin wouldn't exist in the form I do today without you. The journey continues . . .

About TPH

We believe that learning and training are key drivers in achieving the results you want in your life and in your business. We also believe that you shouldn't have to do that all on your own. To that end, we specialize in bringing you compelling ideas from innovative authors who have the expertise to coach you to success. We publish world-class business and talent development content from established experts in the field who share not only their experience and best practices but also the practical tools and resources you—and your organization—need to achieve excellence.

You want to be your best. We want to help.

Visit our website: www.trainerspublishinghouse.com.

Made in the USA
Middletown, DE
26 May 2020